D0660840

Roma 29

GET BY n
ITALIAN

ROSSELLA PERESSINI
ROBERT ANDREWS

LANGUAGE CONSULTANT
ELENA WARD

BBC Active, an imprint of Educational Publishers LLP, part of the Pearson Education Group
Edinburgh Gate, Harlow, Essex CM20 2JE, England.

© Educational Publishers LLP 2007

BBC logo © BBC 1996. BBC and BBC ACTIVE are trademarks of the British Broadcasting
Corporation.

First edition published 1998. This edition published 2007.
Reprinted 2007.

ISBN-13: 978-1-4066-1269-1

Cover design: Emma Wallace
Cover photograph: image100/Punchstock
Insides concept design: Nicolle Thomas
Layout: eMC Design (www.emcdesign.org.uk)
Commissioning editor: Debbie Marshall
Project editor: Melanie Kramers
Project assistant: Hannah Beatson
Senior production controller: Man Fai Lau
Marketing: Fiona Griffiths, Paul East

Printed and bound in the UK.
The Publisher's policy is to use paper manufactured from sustainable forests.

All photographs supplied by Alamy Images.
p8 1StopImages; p10 Travelshots.com; p13 Ian Dagnall; p15 vario images GmbH
& Co.KG; p18 mediacolor's; p25 SAS; p28 Eric Nathan; p30 Sam Toren; p32 Chuck
Pefley; p34 Rough Guides; p38 Michael Belardo; p42 CuboImages srl; p44 Profimedia
International s.r.o.; p47 Paul Carstairs; pp52-53 Mooch Images Limited; p54 Neil
Setchfield; p55 Adam Eastland; p57 travelstock44; p60 Ian Dagnall; p62 Peter Horree;
p65 mediacolor's; p70 Michael Craig; p72 PCL; p76 Nick Simon; p84 Frank Chmura;
p86 Richard Levine; p94 David Ball; p98 Richard Wareham; p101 Jack Sullivan; p102 Neil
Setchfield; p104 Michael Belardo; p107 nagelestock.com; p111 Steven May; p112 Kathy
deWitt; p116 Alan Copson City Pictures; p120 Jack Sullivan.

Contents

How to **use this book**

Get By in Italian is divided into colour-coded topics to help you find what you need quickly. Each unit contains practical travel tips to help you get around and understand the country, and a phrasemaker, to help you say what you need to and understand what you hear.

As well as listing key phrases, **Get By in Italian** aims to help you understand how the language works so that you can build your own phrases and start to communicate independently. The check out dialogues within each section show the language in action, and the try it out activities give you an opportunity to practise for yourself. The link up sections pick out the key structures and give helpful notes about their use. A round-up of all the basic grammar can be found in the Language Builder, pp127-134.

In Italian, all nouns (things, people, concepts) are either masculine or feminine and this affects the way they are written and pronounced as well as the words related to them. In this book alternative word endings are shown: masculine/feminine e.g. sposato/a, meaning married – sposato for a man and sposata for a woman.

If you've bought the pack with the audio CD, you'll be able to listen to a selection of the most important phrases and check out dialogues, as well as all the as if you were there activities. You can use the book on its own – but the CD will help you to improve your pronunciation.

sounds Italian

You don't need perfect pronunciation to be able to communicate – it's enough to get the sound approximately right and to stress words in the correct place. This book uses a pronunciation guide, based on English sounds, to help you start speaking Italian.

stress

A stressed syllable is shown in the pronunciation guide by bold type:

stazione *statsyone*   pizza *pitsa*

In most cases the stress is on the last but one syllable:

amico *ameeko*   amore *amore*

In some longer words, the stress in on the last syllable but two:

vengono *vengono*   camera *kamera*

If there is a written accent, the stress is where the accent is:

città *cheetta*   possibiltà *posseebeelta*

consonants

Many Italian consonants are pronounced in a similar way to English. All doubled consonants are pronounced with an extra long sound.

	sounds like ...	shown as ...
b	'b' in 'but'	*b*
c followed by **e** or **i**	'ch' in 'church'	*ch*
c otherwise	'c' in 'can'	*k*
ch	'c' in 'can'	*k*
d	'd' in 'dog'	*d*
f	'f' in 'feet'	*f*
g followed by **e** or **i**	'j' in 'jet'	*j*
g otherwise	'g' in 'got'	*g*
gh	'g' in 'got'	*g*
gl	'lli' in 'million'	*ly*
gn	'ni' in 'onion'	*ny*
h	always silent	-
j	'y' in 'you'	*y*
l	'l' in 'look'	*l*
m	'm' in 'mat'	*m*
n	'n' in 'not'	*n*
p	'p' in 'pack'	*p*
qu	'qu' in 'quick'	*kw*
r	rolled as in Scottish accent	*r*
rr	strongly rolled	*rr*
s	's' in 'set'	*s*
or sometimes	'z' in 'zoo'	*z*
sc followed by **e** or **i**	'sh' in 'shin'	*sh*
sc otherwise	'sk' in 'skin'	*sk*
t	't' in 'tin'	*t*
v	'v' in 'vain'	*v*
z	'ts' in 'hits'	*ts*
or sometimes	'ds' in 'roads'	*dz*

vowels

Italian vowels are clear and straightforward. For **e** and **o**, there are two slightly different ways of pronouncing each letter, but for simplicity's sake, only one sound is represented in these phrases. A final **e** in a word is always pronounced.

	sounds like ...	shown as ...
a	'a' in 'car'	a
ai	'i' in 'pile'	iy
ao, au	'ow' in 'cow'	ow
e	'e' in 'met'	e
ei	'ay' in 'lay'	e-ee
i	'ee' in 'meet'	ee
or sometimes	'y' in 'yet'	y
o	'o' in 'lot'	o
oi	'oy' in 'boy'	oy
u	'oo' in 'moon'	oo
or sometimes	'w' in 'wobble'	w

alphabet

Here's a guide to how Italians pronounce the alphabet, which may be useful for spelling out your name or an address.

A *ah*	B *bee*	C *chee*	D *dee*
E *eh*	F *effe*	G *jee*	H *akka*
I *ee*	J *ee lunga*	K *kappa*	L *elle*
M *emme*	N *enne*	O *o*	P *pee*
Q *koo*	R *erre*	S *esse*	T *tee*
U *oo*	V *voo*	W *doppia voo*	X *eecs*
Y *ee greca*	Z *dzaytah*		
or *ee eepseelon*			

Bare **Necessities**

phrasemaker

greetings & useful phrases
you may say ...

Hello./Bye. (informal)	Ciao.	*chow*
Good morning.	Buongiorno.	*bwonjorno*
Good afternoon/ evening.	Buonasera.	*bwonasera*
How are things?	Come va?	*kome va*
How are you?	Come sta?	*kome sta*
Fine, and you?	Bene, e lei?	*bene e le-ee*
Not bad.	Non c'è male.	*non che male*
Goodbye. (morning)	Buongiorno.	*bwonjorno*
Goodbye. (evening)	Buonasera.	*bwonasera*
Goodbye. (all day)	Arrivederci.	*arreevederchee*
See you soon!	Ci vediamo!	*chee vedyamo*
See you tomorrow!	A domani!	*a domanee*
Good night.	Buonanotte.	*bwonanotte*
Excuse me. (to get by/attract attention)	permesso/scusi	*permesso/skoozee*
please	per favore/piacere	*per favore/pyachere*
thank you (very much)	grazie (mille)	*gratsye (meelle)*
You're welcome.	Prego.	*prego*
sorry	mi dispiace/scusi	*mee deespyache/ skoozee*
It's all right./It doesn't matter.	Non importa.	*non eemporta*
yes/no	sì/no	*see/no*

is/are there ...?

Is there ... here?	C'è ... qui?	*che ... kwee*
a lift	l'ascensore	*lashensore*
an internet connection	la connessione a internet	*la konnessyone a eenternet*
Are there ...	Ci sono ...	*chee sono*
any toilets?	(delle) toilette/ (i) gabinetti?	*(delle) toylette/ (ee) gabeenettee*

where is/are ...?

Where is ...	Dov'è ...	*dove*
the station?	la stazione?	*la statsyone*
Where are ...	Dove sono ...	*dove sono*
the shoes?	le scarpe?	*le skarpe*
It's ...	È ...	*e*
on the right.	a destra.	*a destra*
on the left.	a sinistra.	*a seeneestra*
straight on.	sempre dritto.	*sempre dreetto*

Bare **Necessities**

you may hear ...

Sono ...	*sono*	They're ...
là.	*la*	there.
in fondo.	*een fondo*	over there.

do you have any ...?
you may say ...

Do you have any ...	Ha ...	*a*
prawns?	dei gamberetti?	*de-ee gamberettee*
tomatoes?	dei pomodori?	*de-ee pomodoree*
strawberries?	delle fragole?	*delle fragole*

how much ...?
you may say ...

How much ...	Quanto ...	*kwanto*
does it cost?	costa?	*kosta*
do they cost?	costano?	*kostano*
How much are ... a kilo?	Quanto costano ... al chilo?	*kwanto kostano ... al keelo*
the tomatoes	i pomodori	*ee pomodoree*
How much is that ... altogether?	Quant'è ... in tutto?	*kwante een tootto*

I'd like ...
you may say ...

I'd like ...	Vorrei ...	*vorre-ee*
a shirt.	una camicia.	*oona kameecha*
a melon.	un melone.	*oon melone*
I'd like ...	Mi dà ...	*mee da*
a kilo of apples.	un chilo di mele?	*oon keelo dee mele*

getting things straight
you may say ...

Pardon?	Come scusi?/Prego?	*kome skoozee/prego*
Can you ...	Può ...	*pwo*
say that again?	ripetere?	*reepetere*
write it down, please?	scriverlo, per favore?	*skreeverlo per favore*
More slowly, please.	Più lentamente, per favore.	*pyoo lentamente per favore*
I (don't) understand.	(Non) capisco.	*(non) kapeesko*
Do you understand?	Capisce?	*kapeeshe*
Do you speak English?	Parla inglese?	*parla eengleze*
How do you spell it?	Come si scrive?	*kome see skreeve*
What does it mean?	Che cosa vuol dire?	*ke koza vwol deere*
I don't know.	Non lo so.	*non lo so*

talking about yourself & others
you may say ...

My name is ...	Mi chiamo ...	*mee kyamo*
I'm ...	Sono ...	*sono*
Mr ...	il signor ...	*eel seenyor*
Mrs ...	la signora ...	*la seenyora*
Miss ...	la signorina ...	*la seenyoreena*
This is ...	Questo è ...	*kwesto e*
Mr ...	il signor ...	*eel seenyor*
my husband.	mio marito.	*mee-o mareeto*
my colleague. (m)	il mio collega.	*eel mee-o kollega*

Bare **Necessities**

This is ...	Questa è ...	*kwesta e*
Mrs ...	la signora ...	*la seenyora*
my wife.	mia moglie.	*mee-a molye*
my colleague. (f)	la mia collega.	*la mee-a kollega*
May I introduce ...	Le presento ...	*le prezento*
Mr ...?	il signor ...	*eel seenyor*
Mrs ...?	la signora ...	*la seenyora*
Pleased to meet you.	Piacere.	*pyachere*
I'm from ...	Sono di ...	*sono dee*
I'm ...	Sono ...	*sono*
English.	inglese.	*eengleze*
Irish.	irlandese.	*eerlandeze*
(nationalities, p18)		
I speak a little Italian.	Parlo un po' d'italiano.	*parlo oon po deetalyano*
I am ...	Sono ...	*sono*
single.	libero/a.	*leebero/a*
married.	sposato/a.	*spozato/a*
separated.	separato/a.	*separato/a*
divorced.	divorziato/a.	*deevortsyato/a*
I have ...	Ho ...	*o*
a partner. (m)	un compagno.	*oon kompanyo*
a partner. (f)	una compagna.	*oona kompanya*
three children.	tre figli.	*tre feelyee*
I'm ... years old.	Ho ... anni.	*o ... annee*
32	trentadue	*trentadoo-e*
(See numbers, p16)		
I work in an office.	Sono impiegato/a.	*sono eempyegato/a*
I'm ...	Sono ...	*sono*
a student. (m)	uno studente.	*oono stoodente*
a student. (f)	una studentessa.	*oona studentessa*
I'm here on ...	Sono qui ...	*sono kwee*
holiday.	in vacanza.	*een vakantsa*
business.	per affari.	*per affaree*
So am I.	Anch'io.	*ankeeo*
I'm staying for ...	Mi fermo ...	*mee fermo*
three days.	tre giorni.	*tre jornee*
a week.	una settimana.	*oona setteemana*

check out 1

You get chatting to another guest in the hotel.

○ Lei è inglese?
  le-ee e eengleze

- No, sono scozzese, di Edinburgo e lei di dov'è?
  no sono scotseze dee edeenboorgo e le-ee dee dove

○ Io sono di Roma. Mi chiamo Bruni. Piacere.
  ee-o sono dee roma. mee kyamo broonee. pyachere

- Piacere – Walker.
  pyachere – walker

○ Quanto si ferma qui a Bellagio?
  kwanto see ferma kwee a bellajo

- Una settimana.
  oona setteemana

Q You are asked whether you are Scottish: true or false?
How long are you staying in Bellagio?

you may hear ...

Come ...	*kome*	What is your name?
ti chiami?	*tee kyamee*	(informal)
si chiama?	*see kyama*	(formal)
Di ...	*dee*	Where are you from?
dove sei?	*dove se-ee*	(informal)
dov'è?	*dee dove*	(formal)
Lei è inglese?	*le-ee e eengleze*	Are you English?
È qui in vacanza?	*e kwee een vakantsa*	Are you here on holiday?
Quanto (tempo) si ferma?	*kwanto (tempo) see ferma*	How long are you staying for?
Che lavoro ...	*ke lavoro*	What do you do?
fai?	*fa-ee*	(informal)
fa?	*fa*	(formal)

Bare **Necessities**

		Are you married?
Sei sposato/a?	*se-ee spozato/a*	(informal)
È sposato/a?	*e spozato/a*	(formal)
		Do you have children?
Hai bambini?	*a-ee bambeenee*	(informal)
Ha bambini?	*a bambeenee*	(formal)
Quanti anni ...	*kwantee annee*	How old are you?
hai?	*a-ee*	(informal)
ha?	*a*	(formal)

check out 2

You continue your conversation with Signor Bruni.

○ Buongiorno, come va?
bwonjorno kome va

- Buongiorno, bene grazie, e lei?
bwonjorno bene gratsye e le-ee

○ Bene, bene ... Signor Bruni, che lavoro fa?
bene bene ... seenyor broonee ke lavoro fa

- Sono impiegato. E lei, che lavoro fa?
sono eempyegato. e le-ee ke lavoro fa

○ Sono uno studente.
sono oono stoodente

Q You work in an office: true or false?

changing money

you may say ...

I'd like to change £100/$100.	Vorrei cambiare cento sterline/ dollari.	*vorre-ee kambyare chento sterleene/ dollaree*
Here you are.	Ecco!	*ekko*
What is ... the exchange rate? the commission charge?	Quant'è ... il cambio? la commissione?	*kwante eel kambyo la kommeessyone*
€7.20	sette euro e venti (centesimi)	*sette e-ooro e ventee (chentezeemee)*
€1.50	un euro e cinquanta	*oon e-ooro e cheenkwanta*

you may hear ...

Mi fa vedere il passaporto?	*mee fa vedere eel passaporto*	May I see your passport?
La commissione è ...	*la kommeessyone e*	The commission charge is ...

check out 3

You need to change some money.

○ Buongiorno, vorrei cambiare cento sterline.
bwonjorno vorre-ee kambyare chento sterleene

- Mi fa vedere il passaporto?
mee fa vedere eel passaporto

○ Ecco ... Quant'è il cambio, per favore?
ekko ... kwante eel kambyo per favore

- La sterlina è a un euro e cinquanta centesimi.
la sterleena e a oon e-ooro e cheenkwanta chentezeemee

Q   What is the exchange rate?

the time

you may say ...

What time is it?	Che ore sono?/ Che ora è?	*ke ore sono/ke ora e*
It's ten past one.	È l'una e dieci.	*e loona e dyechee*
It's quarter past two.	Sono le due e un quarto.	*sono le doo-e e oon kwarto*
It's half past three.	Sono le tre e mezza.	*sono le tre e medza*
It's quarter to four.	Sono le quattro meno un quarto.	*sono le kwattro meno oon kwarto*
It's twenty to six.	Sono le sei meno venti.	*sono le se-ee meno ventee*
What time do you open/close?	A che ora apre/ chiude?	*a ke ora apre/kyoode*
What time does it leave/arrive?	A che ora parte/ arriva?	*a ke ora parte/arreeva*

you may hear ...

Sono le tre.	*sono le tre*	It's three o'clock.
Alle ...	*alle*	At ...
due.	*doo-e*	two o'clock.
dodici e zero otto.	*dodeechee e dzero otto*	12.08.
È ...	*e*	It's ...
mezzogiorno.	*medzojorno*	midday.
mezzanotte.	*medzanotte*	midnight.
l'una.	*loona*	one o'clock.

days

Monday	lunedì	*loonedee*
Tuesday	martedì	*martedee*
Wednesday	mercoledì	*merkoledee*
Thursday	giovedì	*jovedee*
Friday	venerdì	*venerdee*
Saturday	sabato	*sabato*
Sunday	domenica	*domeneeka*
yesterday	ieri	*yeree*
today	oggi	*ojee*
tomorrow	domani	*domanee*

months

January	gennaio	*jenniyo*
February	febbraio	*febbriyo*
March	marzo	*martso*
April	aprile	*apreele*
May	maggio	*majjo*
June	giugno	*joonyo*
July	luglio	*loolyo*
August	agosto	*agosto*
September	settembre	*settembre*
October	ottobre	*ottobre*
November	novembre	*novembre*
December	dicembre	*deechembre*

numbers

0	zero	*dzero*	7	sette	*sette*
1	uno	*oono*	8	otto	*otto*
2	due	*doo-e*	9	nove	*nove*
3	tre	*tre*	10	dieci	*dyechee*
4	quattro	*kwattro*	11	undici	*oondeechee*
5	cinque	*cheenkwe*	12	dodici	*dodeechee*
6	sei	*se-ee*	13	tredici	*tredeechee*

Bare **Necessities**

14	quattordici	*kwattordeechee*	29	ventinove	*venteenove*
15	quindici	*kweendeechee*	30	trenta	*trenta*
16	sedici	*sedeechee*	40	quaranta	*kwaranta*
17	diciassette	*deechassette*	50	cinquanta	*cheenkwanta*
18	diciotto	*deechotto*	60	sessanta	*sessanta*
19	diciannove	*deechannove*	70	settanta	*settanta*
20	venti	*ventee*	80	ottanta	*ottanta*
21	ventuno	*ventoono*	90	novanta	*novanta*
22	ventidue	*venteedoo-e*	100	cento	*chento*
23	ventitré	*venteetre*	101	centouno	*chento-oono*
24	ventiquattro	*venteekwattro*	110	centodieci	*chentodyechee*
25	venticinque	*venteecheenkwe*	200	duecento	*doo-echento*
26	ventisei	*venteese-ee*	1000	mille	*meelle*
27	ventisette	*venteesette*	2000	duemila	*doo-emeela*
28	ventotto	*ventotto*			

ordinal numbers

first	primo/a	*preemo/a*
second	secondo/a	*sekondo/a*
third	terzo/a	*tertso/a*
fourth	quarto/a	*kwarto/a*
fifth	quinto/a	*kweento/a*
sixth	sesto/a	*sesto/a*
seventh	settimo/a	*setteemo/a*
eighth	ottavo/a	*ottavo/a*
ninth	nono/a	*nono/a*
tenth	decimo/a	*decheemo/a*
eleventh	undicesimo/a	*oondeechezeemo/a*
twelfth	dodicesimo/a	*dodeechezeemo/a*

countries & nationalities

Australia: Australian	Australia: australiano/a	*owstralya: owstralyano/a*
Canada: Canadian	Canada: canadese	*kanada: kanadeze*
England: English	Inghilterra: inglese	*engeelterra: eengleze*
France: French	Francia: francese	*francha: francheze*
Germany: German	Germania: tedesco/a	*jermanya: tedesko/a*
Great Britain: British	Gran Bretagna: britannico/a	*gran bretanya: britanneeko/a*
Ireland: Irish	Irlanda: irlandese	*eerlanda: eerlandeze*
Italy: Italian	Italia: italiano/a	*eetalya: italyano/a*
New Zealand: New Zealander	Nuova Zelanda: neozelandese	*nwova dzelanda: ne-o-dzelandeze*
Russia: Russian	Russia: russo/a	*roossee-a: roossolo/a*
Scotland: Scottish	Scozia: scozzese	*skotsya: skotseze*
South Africa: South African	Sudafrica: sudafricano/a	*sood-afrika: sood-afrikano/a*
Spain: Spanish	Spagna: spagnolo/a	*spanya: spanyolo/a*
Switzerland: Swiss	Svizzera: svizzero/a	*sveetsera: sveetsero/a*
United States: American	Stati Uniti: americano/a	*statee ooneetee: amerikano/a*
Wales: Welsh	Galles: gallese	*galles: galleze*

Bare **Necessities**

sound check

In Italian, the pronunciation of the vowels **a**, **i** and **u** is very straightforward.

a sounds like the 'a' in 'park':

casa *kaza*

i like the 'ee' in 'sheep':

vino *veeno*

u like the 'oo' in 'tool':

uva *oova*

e and **o** are slightly more complicated, as they can have two different pronunciations.

e can be open, like the 'e' in 'pen', or closed, more like the 'a' in 'base':

terra *terra*   pera *pera*

o can have an open sound, like the 'o' in 'hot', or a closed sound, more like 'oa' in 'load':

pollo *pollo*   noce *noache*

try it out

question time

Match the questions 1–5 with the correct responses a–e.

1 Dov'è la stazione?
2 A che ora apre la banca?
3 Di dov'è lei?
4 Come sta?
5 Quanto costa?

a Bene, grazie, e lei?
b Sono di Venezia.
c È sempre dritto.
d Sette euro.
e Alle due e mezza.

as if you were there

On holiday, you get talking to a fellow parent while your children are playing in the hotel pool. Follow the prompts to play your part.

Buongiorno!

(Say good morning)

Mi chiamo Aldo, e lei?

(Tell him your name is Anna and you are from Edinburgh)

È sposata?

(Say yes, you are married. Your husband's name is James and he is Scottish)

Ah ... ha due bambini, no?

(Say no, one daughter, Julia)

(Now ask him how many children he has)

Ho due bambini, Benedetta e Enrico. Eccoli lì! A presto!

Bare **Necessities**

linkup

Mi chiamo ...	**My name is** ...
Sono inglese.	**I'm** English.
Sono di Londra.	**I'm from** London.
Ho due bambini.	**I have** two children.
Ci sono (delle) toilette?	**Are there** any toilets?
Dov'è la stazione?	**Where's** the station?
Vorrei un chilo di mele.	**I'd like** a kilo of apples.

the way you say things

You can't always transfer things word for word from English to Italian. For example, Mi chiamo Anna (My name is Anna) literally means 'Myself I call Anna'. So sometimes it pays to learn the whole phrase rather than the individual words.

listening & replying

When people ask you questions about yourself, such as Ha bambini? (Do you have children?), it's tempting to reply using the same word: ha. Instead, you must change the form of the verb 'to have', using ho (I have) not ha (you have):

Sì, **ho** bambini./No, **non ho** bambini.   Yes, I have children./ No, I don't have children.

Some other common questions and possible replies:

Dove **vive**? – **Vivo** a Edinburgo.   Where do you live? – I live in Edinburgh.
Come **ti chiami**? – **Mi chiamo** Anna.   What's your name? – My name is Anna.

missing words

Because the form of the verb tells you who is being referred to, it's very common in Italian not to use the words for I (io), you (tu), etc.

Vivo a Edinburgo. (not Io vivo) I live in Edinburgh.

Ho due bambini. (not Io ho) I have two children.

The same applies to the words for he, she (lui, lei) and it:

Come si chiama la sua bambina? – **Si chiama** Julia. (not Lei si chiama Julia)
What's your daughter called? – She's called Julia.

Come si chiama suo marito? – **Si chiama** James. (not Lui si chiama James)
What's your husband called? – He's called James.

talking to people

There are three ways of saying 'you' in Italian:
Lei (occasionally spelled with a capital) when you don't know the person very well
tu to a friend or a younger person
voi when you are talking to two or more people

This book uses mainly lei.

Lei parl**a** inglese? Do you speak English?
Lei viv**e** a Edinburgo? Do you live in Edinburgh?

The word you choose for 'you' changes the ending of the verb. In the present tense, with lei, the verb often ends in **-a** or **-e**.

For more on talking to people , see the Language Builder, p128. ········▷

Getting **Around**

by air

Italy's national airline, Alitalia, links all major Italian cities using two hub airports, Rome Fiumicino and Milan Malpensa. All the airports have regular bus or train connections to the city centre.

by car

Driving in Italy can be a stressful experience, with congestion and lack of parking a problem. Petty car-crime is also common. The historical centre of the majority of towns is closed to traffic. Car documentation should be carried at all times, including your driving licence. You must pay a toll to travel on the **autostrade** (motorways) – take a ticket on joining the motorway, pay when you exit, by cash or credit card. The motorway speed limit is 80mph, or 70mph for cars with engines of less than 1100cc. Petrol stations on motorways are open 24 hours a day, and most have automatic self-service pumps which accept €10 and €20 notes.

In small towns and rural areas they tend to open 7am–12.30pm and 3.30pm–7.30pm, except on Sundays (mornings only).

car hire

Hiring a car is generally cheaper if arranged before you travel. All major international car hire firms have offices at airports and city railway stations. A national driving licence and passport are the only documents required, while credit cards are the preferred method of payment. You can also hire scooters in most towns, a good way to see local sights.

by train

Italian rail is a convenient and cheap way to cover long distances. Smoking is not permitted on any train. The main train types are:

Treni Eurostar Italia Alta Velocità These fast, comfortable trains link the main cites in Italy in style, but can be expensive.

Intercity Fast trains linking Italian cities. Seat reservation is required and there is a small supplement to pay.

Interregionale, Espresso and Diretto The most common trains, referred to by all three names. These are cheaper than Intercity services, but not as fast, as they stop at provincial towns.

Regionale and Locale Local trains covering shorter distances and stopping at every station.

Reservation is recommended for all trains. You can buy tickets online, at the station from the **biglietteria** (ticket office), or with a credit card from an automatic machine. Tickets must be validated at small yellow machines near the platforms before boarding. For ticket and timetable information, visit **www.trenitalia.com**.

Some trains don't run all the time: check the timetable for restrictions, marked **stagionale** or **periodico**. Rail fares in Italy are based on the distance travelled, so if planning to make a lot of journeys get a Trenitalia Pass, which allows unlimited rail travel for four to ten consecutive days within a two-month period. There are further discounts available for young people and senior citizens. Children under four travel free, and those under 11 at half price.

by coach

Travel by **pullman** (coach) tends to be pricier than train travel, though schedules are generally more reliable. Major towns have a central **autostazione** (bus station) where you can buy tickets. In smaller towns, you may have to purchase tickets at a bar near the coach stop, or on board.

taxis

Taxis can be expensive, especially for journeys to or from airports. Choose only official taxis (those with 'Taxi' on the roof) and fix a price beforehand for long journeys. Supplements are added for luggage, being ordered by phone and journeys out of town, on Sundays, on public holidays and at night.

ferries & hydrofoils

You will need to take to the water to reach Italy's many outlying islands. The **traghetto** (ferry), **aliscafo** (hydrofoil) and **vaporetto** (water bus) are an integral part of the Italian transport system, not just on Venice's canals.

Getting **Around**

buses, trams & funiculars

City buses and trams are cheap and frequent, though they can also be unbearably crowded and in summer you may prefer to walk. There is an efficient night service in most towns, with hourly departures. Funiculars are a useful way of travelling in places like Naples or Orvieto. **Biglietti** (tickets) must be purchased before travel and immediately validated once on board. Usually, the same ticket can be re-used on the bus, tram or funicular and underground and is valid for 60 or 75 minutes after being stamped (but check locally).

They are obtainable from **tabacchini** (tobacconist's) and some bars, as well as bus station kiosks. You can buy booklets of ten single tickets, or, in some places, one-day passes.

metropolitana

Rome, Naples and Milan all have useful (if limited) underground railway systems. Milan has three lines meeting at the Stazione Centrale, while Rome has just two lines, again converging on the main rail station (Termini), and Naples only one. Services stop at around 11pm. Note that Naples also has a useful private railway line linking Herculaneum, Pompeii and Sorrento.

phrasemaker

asking the way
you may say ...

Excuse me!	Scusi!	*skoozee*
Where/Which way is ...	Dov'è ...	*dove*
the station?	la stazione?	*la statsyone*
the tourist office?	l'ufficio del turismo?	*looffeecho del tooreezmo*
the bus stop?	la fermata dell'autobus?	*la fermata dellowtobus*
Is it far?	È lontano?	*e lontano*
Is there ... near here?	C'è ... qui vicino?	*che ... kwee veecheeno*
a bank	una banca	*oona banka*
a cashpoint	un bancomat	*oon bankomat*
a car park	un parcheggio	*oon parkejjo*
Are there any ... near here?	Ci sono ... qui vicino?	*chee sono ... kwee vecheeno*
toilets	toilette	*toylette*
shops	negozi	*negotsee*
Is this the right way to ...	Questa è la strada per ...	*kwesta e la strada per*
the town centre?	il centro?	*eel chentro*
the airport?	l'aeroporto?	*la-eroporto*

you may hear ...

Dunque/Allora ...	*doonkwe/allora*	Well/Right ...
È là.	*e la*	There it is./It's over there.
Giri a destra/sinistra.	*jeeree a destra/ seeneestra*	Turn right/left.
dopo il semaforo	*dopo eel semaforo*	after the traffic lights
Poi attraversi ...	*po-ee attraversee*	Then cross ...
il ponte.	*eel ponte*	the bridge.
la strada.	*la strada*	the road.

Getting **Around**

la prima/seconda	la *preema/sekonda*	the first/second
sulla destra/sinistra	*soolla destra/seeneestra*	on the right/left
Vada sempre dritto.	*vada sempre dreetto*	Carry straight on.
fino all'incrocio	*feeno aleenkrocho*	as far as the crossroads
a cento metri	*a chento metree*	100 metres away
in fondo alla strada	*een fondo alla strada*	at the end of the street
dietro l'angolo	*dyetro langolo*	round/on the corner
È abbastanza ...	*e abbastantsa*	It's quite ...
vicino.	*veecheeno*	near.
lontano.	*lontano*	far away.
di fronte ...	*dee fronte*	opposite ...
al museo	*al mooze-o*	the museum
alla chiesa	*alla kyeza*	the church
dietro la banca	*dyetro la banka*	behind the bank

(For a list of shops, see p55, and for places to visit, see p99)

check out 1

You are looking for an internet café.

○ Scusi, dov'è il punto internet?
skoozee dove eel poonto eenternet

- Allora, vada sempre dritto, dopo il semaforo la seconda a destra.
alora vada sempre dreetto dopo eel semaforo la sekonda a destra

○ È lontano?
e lontano

- No, a cento metri.
no a chento metree

Q The internet café is straight on, then after the traffic lights, the second turning on the left: true or false?

hiring a car or bike

you may say ...

I'd like to hire a ...	Vorrei noleggiare ...	*vorre-ee nolejjare*
car.	una macchina.	*oona makeena*
scooter.	un motorino.	*oon motoreeno*
motorbike.	una moto.	*oona moto*
a small/medium/big car	una macchina piccola/media/grande	*oona makkeena peekkola/medya/grande*
for ...	per ...	*per*
three days	tre giorni	*tre jornee*
a week	una settimana	*oona setteemana*
How much is it ...	Quanto costa ...	*kwanto kosta*
per day?	al giorno?	*al jorno*
a week?	alla settimana?	*alla setteemana*
Is insurance included?	È inclusa l'assicurazione?	*e eenklooza lasseekooratsyone*

you may hear ...

Per quanto tempo?	*per kwanto tempo*	For how long?
Mi fa vedere ... per favore?	*mee fa vedere ... per favore*	Can I see your ... please?
la patente	*la patente*	driving licence
il passaporto	*eel passaporto*	passport
La cauzione è di ... euro.	*la kaootsyone e dee ... e-ooro*	The deposit is ... euros. (See numbers, p16)

check out 2
You want to hire a small car.

- ○ Buongiorno, vorrei noleggiare una macchina piccola. Quanto costa al giorno?
  bwonjorno vorre-ee nolejjare oona makkeena peekkola. kwanto kosta al jorno

- Novanta euro al giorno. Per quanto tempo?
  novanta e-ooro al jorno. per kwanto tempo

- ○ Per una settimana. È inclusa l'assicurazione?
  per oona setteemana. e eenklooza lasseekooratsyone

- Sì. C'è una cauzione di duecento euro.
  see. che oona kaootsyone dee doo-echento e-ooro

Q The car costs €90 a day: true or false?
Is insurance included?

getting petrol
you may say ...

Where is the ...	Dov'è ...	*dove*
unleaded?	la benzina senza piombo?	*la bentseena sentsa pyombo*
diesel?	il diesel?	*eel deezel*
4-star?	il super?	*eel sooper*
Where is the air?	Dov'è la pompa d'aria, per favore?	*dove la pompa daree-a per favore*

on the road
you may say ...

Is this the road to ...?	Questa è la strada per ...?	*kwesta e la strada per*
How far is it to ...?	Quanto è distante ...?	*kwanto e deestante*
Where is ...?	Per ...?	*per*

(For breakdowns, see Emergencies, p122)

getting information

you may say ...

Are there buses/ trains to ...?	Ci sono autobus/treni per ...?	*chee sono awtoboos/ trenee per*
What time does the bus ... leave? arrive?	A che ora ... l'autobus? parte arriva	*a ke ora ... lawtoboos parte arreeva*
What time does the next one leave?	A che ora parte il prossimo?	*a ke ora parte eel prosseemo*
From which platform?	Da che binario?	*da ke beenaryo*
Is there wheelchair access?	C'è l'accesso per la sedia a rotelle?	*che lachesso per la sedya a rotelle*
Is it direct?	È diretto?	*e deeretto*
What time is the connection?	A che ora è la coincidenza?	*a ke ora e la coencheedentsa*
Have you got a timetable?	Ha un orario?	*a oon oraryo*
Where is the ticket office, please?	Dov'è la biglietteria, per favore?	*dove la beelyettereea per favore*
Does this train go to ...?	Questo treno va a ...?	*kwesto treno va a*
Where do I need to get off?	Dove devo scendere?	*dove devo shendere*
Which line goes to ...?	Che linea per ...?	*ke leenea per*

you may hear ...

C'è un treno ogni ora.	che oon **treno** onyee ora	There's a train every hour.

fra/tra ...
  un quarto d'ora
  mezz'ora
	fra/tra
	  oon **kwa**rto dora
	  me**dzo**ra
		in ...
		  quarter of an hour
		  half an hour
		(See times, p15)

Prenda la linea/il numero ...	**pren**da la **lee**nea/eel **noo**mero	Take line/number ...

Deve cambiare/scendere ...
  fra due fermate.
  alla prossima.
	deve kam**bya**re/**shen**dere
	  fra **doo**-e fer**ma**te
	  alla **pro**sseema
		You have to change/get off ...
		  in two stops.
		  at the next stop.

Le faccio vedere.	le **fa**cho ve**de**re	I'll show you.

check out 3

You are travelling to Venice by bus.

○ Questo autobus va a Venezia?
  kwesto **aw**toboos va a ve**ne**tsya

- Sì.
  see

○ Dove devo scendere?
  dove **de**vo **shen**dere

- Deve scendere fra due fermate.
  deve **shen**dere fra **doo**-e fer**ma**te

Q You need to get off at the next stop: true or false?

buying tickets

A book of tickets.	Un blocchetto di biglietti.	*oon bloketto dee beelyettee*

a ... ticket
  single
  return
	un biglietto ...
	  solo andata
	  andata e ritorno
		*oon beelyetto
		  solo andata
		  andata e reetorno*

For two adults and one child.	Per due adulti e un bambino.	*per doo-e adooltee e oon bambeeno*
1st/2nd class	prima/seconda classe	*preema/sekonda klasse*

Are there discounts for ...
  students?
  senior citizens?
  travellers with disabilities?
	Ci sono sconti per ...
	  studenti?
	  anziani?
	  disabili?
		*chee sono skontee per
		  stoodentee
		  antsyanee
		  deezabeelee*

I'd like to reserve ...
  a seat.
  a couchette.
	Vorrei prenotare ...
	  un posto.
	  una cuccetta.
		*vorre-ee prenotare
		  oon posto
		  oona koochetta*

Cinque euro di supplemento Intercity.	*cheenkwe e-ooro dee soopplemento interseetee*	There's an Intercity supplement of €5.

Getting **Around**

signs
you may see ...

accettazione	check-in
arrivi	arrivals
binario	platform
controllo di sicurezza	security check
controllo passaporti	passport control
convalidare il biglietto	validate your ticket
deposito bagagli	left-luggage office
dogana	customs
partenze	departures
uscita	gate, exit
vietato attraversare i binari	do not cross the tracks
vietato sporgersi dal finestrino	do not lean out of the window
vietato fumare	no smoking

taking a taxi
you may say ...

Is there a taxi rank near here?	C'è un posteggio di taxi qui vicino?	*che oon postejjo dee taksee kwee veecheeno*
To the airport, please.	L'aeroporto, per favore.	*la-eroporto per favore*
To this address, please.	Questo indirizzo, per favore.	*kwesto eendeereetso, per favore*
Is it far?	È lontano?	*e lontano*
How long will it take?	Quanto tempo ci vuole?	*kwanto tempo chee vwole*
Keep the change.	Tenga il resto.	*tenga eel resto*
This is for you.	Questo è per lei.	*kwesto e per le-ee*
Could I have a receipt, please?	Mi dà la ricevuta, per favore?	*mee da la reechevoota per favore*

check out 4

You're taking a taxi to the airport.

○ L'aeroporto, per favore. Quanto costa?
*la-ero**po**rto per fa**vo**re. **kwa**nto **ko**sta*

- Trentacinque euro.
*trenta**cheen**kwe **e**-ooro*

○ Quanto tempo ci vuole?
***kwa**nto **te**mpo chee **vwo**le*

- Venti minuti.
***ven**tee mee**noo**tee*

(later)

○ Ecco – e questo è per lei. Mi dà la ricevuta, per favore?
***ek**ko – e **kwe**sto e per **le**-ee. mee da la reeche**voo**ta per
fa**vo**re*

Q It takes 35 minutes to get to the airport: true or false?
How much do you pay?

Getting **Around**

sound check

c is pronounced in two ways, depending on the letter that follows it.

c + **e** or **i** sounds like 'ch' in 'church':

cena *chena*   cinque *cheenkwe*

c + anything else sounds like 'c' in 'cool':

camera *kamera*   costano *kostano*
bicchiere *beekkyere*   che *ke*

Practise on these words:

città *cheetta*   mi chiamo *mee kyamo*

try it out

mind the gap
Complete these sentences with the words on the right.

1 Quanto costa un ...?   **a** fermata
2 Dopo il ... a destra.   **b** ritorno
3 C'è un ... qui vicino?   **c** semaforo
4 Dov'è la ... dell'autobus?   **d** biglietto
5 Andata e ...   **e** punto internet

as if you were there
You're at the train station to buy tickets to Venice, for you and your partner. Follow the prompts to play your part.

Prego?

(Ask for two return tickets to Venice)

Diciasette euro e cinque di supplemento Intercity.

(Ask what time the train leaves)

Alle dieci e zero otto.

(Ask whether it is a direct train)

No, deve cambiare a Padova.

(Ask what time the connection is)

Dunque, il treno arriva a Padova alle dodici e trenta e la coincidenza è alle tredici e zero cinque.

(Thank him)

key phrases

Dov'è il punto internet?	**Where/Which way is** the internet café?
È lontano?	**Is it** far?
C'è un bancomat qui vicino?	**Is there** a cashpoint near here?
Ci sono negozi qui vicino?	**Are there** any shops near here?
Vorrei noleggiare una macchina.	**I'd like** to hire a car.
A che ora parte il treno?	**What time** does the train leave?

how to ask a question

Asking questions is simple in Italian. Change your intonation at the end of a sentence to turn a statement into a question:

Il vaporetto arriva fra venti minuti. The water bus arrives in 20 minutes.
Il vaporetto arriva fra venti minuti? Does the water bus arrive in 20 minutes?

Note that Italian has no equivalent of the English use of 'do' or 'does' in questions.

Many questions also follow the same word order as in English:

Dov'è la stazione? **Where is** the station?
Quant'è il biglietto? **How much is** the ticket?
Quando arriva? **When** does it arrive

For more on questions, see the Language Builder, p131. ·····⋗

masculine or feminine?

In Italian all nouns (words for things, places, people, concepts) are either masculine or feminine.

In the singular form, most nouns end in **-o** or **-a** (and some in **-e**). Almost all those ending in **-o** are masculine (il treno, il biglietto) and almost all those ending in **-a** are feminine (la macchina, l'autostrada).

There's no hard and fast rule for words ending in **-e**, so it's a good idea to learn the gender (masculine or feminine) of each one as you learn the word. But don't worry if you get it wrong. You'll usually be understood!

For more on gender, see the Language Builder, p127. ⤳

asking the way

When you are looking for something, you'll need to use the expressions dove (where) and dov'è ...? (where is ...?). Although they look very similar, there's a difference in pronunciation: the stress in dove is on the first syllable: *dove* and in dov'è the stress is on the last syllable: *dove*.

Dove va questo vaporetto? **Where** does this waterbus go?
Dov'è il punto internet? **Where is** the internet café?

When asking how far away somewhere is, use lontano or lontana:

È **lontano** il bancomat? Is the cashpoint far? (because il bancomat is masculine)
È **lontana** la stazione? Is the station far? (because la stazione is feminine)

You might hear:

Sì, è **abbastanza** lontano. Yes, it's **quite** far.
No, è **vicino**. No, it's **nearby**.

Somewhere **to Stay**

where to stay

Italy has a wide range of hotels, apartments, **agriturismo** (rural tourism) facilities, ski resorts and campsites. If you arrive in town without a reservation, ask for advice at the tourist office. It can provide a list of local accommodation and may be able to phone for you to check availability and prices. Most types of accommodation cater for children of all ages, but it's advisable to check beforehand. They will often put an extra bed in your room for an additional 30-40% of the price of the room.

hotels & guesthouses

Hotel accommodation is categorised by stars, from one (cheapest) to five (most expensive). Three or more stars will generally include a telephone and en suite facilities.

In high season, many hotels insist on visitors paying for half or full board. If you can avoid rates which include breakfast, you'll find it cheaper and better in local bars. A **pensione** is similar to a B&B, and is often family-run with plenty of character.

self-catering & farm holidays

Self-catering can be a much cheaper and more satisfying alternative to hotel accommodation. Villas and apartments are best booked through an agency before leaving.

If you are looking for peace and quiet in the Italian countryside, the **agriturismo** scheme offers the chance to stay in self-catering cottages or farmhouses, see: **www.agriturismo.it** for details. Other options may include half or full board. Many cottages have swimming pools and offer country pursuits such as horseriding, as well as the chance to buy farm produce.

youth hostels & campsites

Italy has a good distribution of youth hostels, but they are more sparse south of Rome. Find one at: **www.iyhf.org**. Hostels are usually located a bus ride away from the city centres. In most cases you must hold a current HI (Hostelling International) card (sometimes obtainable from the hostel) or take out temporary membership; in some private hostels this is not necessary.

Hikers will appreciate the **rifugi** (mountain huts) situated along walking routes, often in highly scenic locations. Ask at the tourist office about availability and terms, or look up the Club Alpino Italiano: **www.cai.it**.

Camping is a popular option, especially on the coasts. Sites can become extremely crowded in summer and advance booking is recommended. Some campsites have huts or small bungalows for rent as well as tents, and most have bars, restaurants and shops; pools and nightclubs are often found in the bigger ones. The local tourist office will have a list of sites in the vicinity. Note that many campsites close between September and Easter and that camping outside official sites is illegal.

phrasemaker

places to stay

bed and breakfast	la pensione	*la pensyone*
hotel	l'albergo	*lalbergo*
youth hostel	l'ostello	*lostello*
campsite	il campeggio	*eel kampejjo*
holiday village	il villaggio turistico	*eel veelajo tooreesteeko*
to let ...	affittansi ...	*affeettansee*
villas	villette	* veellette*
apartments	appartamenti	* appartamentee*
rooms	stanze	* stantse*

finding a place & checking in

you may say ...

Is there a hotel near here?	C'è un albergo qui vicino?	*che oon albergo kwee veecheeno*
Do you have a single/double room?	Ha una camera singola/doppia?	*a oona kamera seengola/doppya*
with ...	con ...	*kon*
a double bed	letto matrimoniale	* letto matreemonyale*
twin beds	due letti	* doo-e lettee*
a cot	un lettino	* oon letteeno*
I have a reservation.	Ho prenotato.	*o prenotato*
It's in the name of ...	È a nome di ...	*e a nome dee*
My name is ...	Mi chiamo ...	*mee kyamo*
For ...	Per ...	*per*
four people.	quattro persone.	* kwattro persone*
two adults and two children.	due adulti e due bambini.	* doo-e adooltee e doo-e bambeenee*
three nights.	tre notti.	* tre nottee*
one week.	una settimana.	* oona setteemana*
How much is it per night?	Quanto costa per notte?	*kwanto kosta per notte*
Do you have anything cheaper?	Ha qualcosa di meno caro?	*a kwalkoza dee meno karo*

Somewhere to Stay

Are there any special rates for children?	Ci sono riduzioni per bambini?	_chee sono reedootsyo-nee per bambeenee_
Is breakfast included?	La prima colazione è inclusa?	_la preema kolatsyone e eenklooza?_
Do you have wheelchair-accessible rooms?	Avete camere per i clienti con sedia a rotelle?	_avete kamere per ee klee-entee kon sedya a rotelle_
May I see the room?	Posso vedere la camera?	_posso vedere la kamera_
Fine, I'll take it.	Va bene, la prendo.	_va bene la prendo_
I'll think about it.	Ci penso.	_chee penso_
Where can I park?	Dove posso parcheggiare?	_dove posso parkejjare_

you may hear ...

Per quante notti?	_per kwante nottee_	How many nights?
Per quante persone?	_per kwante persone_	How many people?
Mi dispiace, è tutto occupato/siamo al completo.	_mee deespyache e tootto okkoopato/syamo al kompleto_	Sorry, we're full.
I bambini pagano metà.	_ee bambeenee pagano meta_	Children pay half price.
Che nome?	_ke nome_	What name?
Mi dà il passaporto, per favore?	_mee da eel passaporto per favore_	Can I have your passport, please?
Può compilare la scheda, per favore?	_pwo kompeelare la skeda per favore_	Can you fill in the form, please?
Camera numero ...	_kamera noomero_	Room number ...
Il parcheggio è dietro, a sinistra.	_eel parkejjo e dyetro a seeneestra_	The car park is at the back, on the left.
Che numero di targa ha?	_ke noomero dee targa a_	What's your car registration?
... si paga a parte. La colazione La tassa di soggiorno	_... see paga a parte la kolatsyone la tassa dee sojjorno_	... is extra. Breakfast Visitors' tax
mezza pensione	_medza pensyone_	half board
pensione completa	_pensyone kompleta_	full board

check out 1

You are at a hotel reception, asking whether they have a single room available.

○ Buongiorno, ha una camera singola?
bwonjorno a oona kamera seengola

- Per quante notti?
per kwante nottee

○ Per due notti. Quanto costa per notte?
per doo-e nottee. kwanto kosta per notte

- Centocinque euro per notte.
chentocheenkwe e-ooro per notte

Q How many nights do you want to stay?
How much is the total cost?

asking about your room

you may say ...

Does the room have ...	La camera ha ...	la kamera a
a bath?	un bagno?	oon banyo
a shower?	una doccia?	oona docha
When do I have to check out?	Quando devo liberare la camera?	kwando devo leeberare la kamera
What time is ...	A che ora è la ...	a ke ora e la
breakfast?	prima colazione?	preema kolatsyone
dinner?	cena?	chena
Is there ...	C'è ...	che
a lift?	l'ascensore?	lashensore
air conditioning?	il condizionatore?	il kondeetsyonatore
an internet connection in the room?	la connessione a internet in camera?	la konnessyone a eenternet een kamera
Do you have an ...	Ha un ...	a oon
adapter?	riduttore?	reedoottore
iron?	ferro da stiro?	ferro da steero
Where is the ...	Dov'è ...	dove
restaurant?	il ristorante?	eel reestorante
bar?	il bar?	eel bar
gym?	la palestra?	la palestra
conference room?	la sala conferenze?	la sala konferentse
How do I get an outside number?	Come faccio per telefonare fuori?	kome facho per telefonare fworee?

you may hear ...

Dalle sette e mezza alle dieci e mezza.	dalle sette e medza alle dyechee e medza	From 7.30 to 10.30.
È al ... piano.	e al ... pyano	It's on the ... floor.
primo	preemo	first
secondo	sekondo	second
terzo	tertso	third
al pianterreno	al pyanterreno	on the ground floor
Faccia lo zero.	facha lo dzero	Dial zero.

check out 2

You're asking about a cheaper room.

○ Quanto costa?
  kwanto kosta

- Centocinque euro per notte, la colazione si paga
  a parte sei euro.
  *chentocheenkwe e-ooro per notte la kolatsyone see paga
  a parte se-ee e-ooro*

○ Ha qualcosa di meno caro?
  a kwalkoza dee meno karo

- No, mi dispiace.
  no mee deespyache

○ Posso vedere la camera?
  posso vedere la kamera

- Prego.
  prego

Q   Is breakfast included?

Somewhere to Stay

problems

you may say ...

... isn't working.	... non funziona.	... non foontsyona
The telephone	Il telefono	eel telefono
The shower	La doccia	la docha
There is a problem with ...	Ho un problema con ...	o oon problema kon
the lock.	la serratura.	la serratoora
How do you work ...	Come funziona ...	kome foontsyona
the heating?	il riscaldamento?	eel reeskaldamento
the TV?	il televisore?	eel televeezore
There's no ...	Manca ...	manka
hot water.	l'acqua calda.	lakwa kalda
soap.	il sapone.	eel sapone
toilet paper.	la carta igienica.	la karta eejeneeka
There are (also) no ...	Mancano (anche) ...	mankano (anke)
towels.	gli asciugamani.	lee ashoogamanee
pillows.	i cuscini.	ee koosheenee
blankets.	le coperte.	le koperte

you may hear ...

Che cosa c'è?	ke koza che	What's the problem?
Basta ...	basta	All you have to do is ... it.
tirare.	teerare	pull
spingere.	speenjere	push
girare.	jeerare	turn
Tirare verso ...	teerare verso	Pull it ...
l'alto.	lalto	upwards.
il basso.	eel basso	downwards.
destra.	destra	to the right.
sinistra.	seeneestra	to the left.
Mando qualcuno.	mando kwalkoono	I'll send somebody.
Glieli/le porto subito.	lyelee/le porto soobeeto	I'll bring you some now.

asking for help

you may say ...

Could I have an alarm call at ...?	Vorrei la sveglia per ...	*vorre-ee la svelya per*
Do you have a map of the town?	Ha una pianta della città?	*a oona pyanta della cheetta*
Is there a ...	C'è ...	*che*
safe?	una cassaforte?	*oona kassaforte*
safe deposit box?	una cassetta di sicurezza?	*oona kassetta dee seekooretsa*
Can you ...	Mi può ...	*mee pwo*
recommend a good restaurant?	consigliare un buon ristorante?	*konseelyare oon bwon reestorante*
order me a taxi?	chiamare un taxi?	*kyamare oon taksee*

checking out

you may say ...

I'd like to pay the bill, please.	Vorrei il conto, per favore.	*vorre-ee eel konto per favore*
Can I pay ...	Posso pagare ...	*posso pagare*
by credit card?	con la carta di credito?	*kon la karta dee kredeeto*
with cash?	in contanti?	*een kontantee*
I think there is a mistake.	C'è un errore, credo.	*che oon errore kredo*

you may hear ...

Qual è il numero della stanza/camera?	*kwale eel noomero della stantsa/kamera*	What is your room number?
Come vuole pagare?	*kome vwole pagare*	How would you like to pay?
Mi fa il numero di codice?	*mee fa eel noomero dee kodeeche*	Can you enter your PIN?
Può firmare qui, per favore?	*pwo feermare kwee, per favore*	Can you sign here, please?
Vediamo ... Sì, ha ragione.	*veedyamo. see a rajone*	Let's see ... Yes, you're right.

check out 3

Time to check out and pay the bill.

- ○ Vorrei il conto, per favore.
  vorre-ee eel konto per favore

- – Qual è il numero della stanza?
  kwale eel noomero della stantsa

- ○ Settantadue. Posso pagare con la carta di credito?
  settantadoo-e. posso pagare kon la karta dee kredeeto

- – Certo. Mi fa il numero di codice, per favore?
  cherto. mee fa eel noomero dee kodeeche per favore

Q What two questions are you asked?

at the youth hostel

you may say …

Do you have …	Ha …	
a bed?	un letto?	*oon letto*
a family room?	una stanza per famiglia?	*oona stantsa per fameelya*
Can I hire …	Posso noleggiare …	*posso nolejare*
a sleeping bag?	un sacco a pelo?	*oon sakko a pelo*
some sheets?	delle lenzuola?	*delle lentsuola*
What time do you lock up?	A che ora chiudete la porta?	*a ke ora kyoodete la porta*

you may hear …

È socio/socia?	*e socho/socha*	Do you have an HI membership card?

47

campsites

Have you got space for a …	Ha posto per una …	*a posto per oona*
caravan?	roulotte?	*roolot*
tent?	tenda?	*tenda*
How much is it …	Quanto si paga …	*kwanto see paga*
per person?	per persona?	*per persona*
a day?	al giorno?	*al jorno*
Is there …	C'è …	*che*
a launderette?	una lavanderia?	*oona lavandereea*
a supermarket?	un supermercato?	*oon soopermerkato*
Where are the …	Dove sono …	*dove sono*
showers?	le docce?	*le doche*
dustbins?	i cassonetti?	*ee kassonettee*
toilets?	le toilette?	*le toylette*

you may hear …

Abbiamo una piazzola per tre notti.	*abbyamo oona pyatsola per tre nottee*	We have a pitch free for three nights.
Costa quindici euro per notte.	*kosta kweendeechee e-ooro per notte*	It costs €15 per night.

sound check

When s comes before **ce** or **ci**, the pronunciation changes.

s + **ce** or **ci** is pronounced like the 'sh' in 'ship':

scelta *shelta* sciopero *shopero*

Practise on these words:

asciugamano *ashoogamano* lasciare *lashare*

ascensore *ashensore* scendere *shendere*

strisce *streeshe* uscire *oosheere*

try it out

in the mix

Unscramble the words in capitals to complete the sentences.

1   Scusi, c'è una SASACORTEF nell'albergo?
2   Scusi, manca la TARAC CIANIEGI nella stanza 31.
3   Scusi, come funziona il VITEROSELE?
4   Scusi, ho un problema con la SARRUTERA.
5   Scusi, mancano gli NIMAGASCIUA, nella stanza 32.

question time

Match each question on the left with the correct answer on the right – all things you might say or hear in a hotel.

1	Ha una camera singola?	a	Due adulti e due bambini.
2	Ha qualcosa di meno caro?	b	No, si paga a parte.
3	Che nome per favore?	c	Mi dispiace, è tutto occupato.
4	Quanto costa per notte?	d	Smith.
5	Per quante persone?	e	No, mi dispiace.
6	La prima colazione è inclusa?	f	€45.

as if you were there

Imagine you're in a hotel reception, asking about a room. Follow the prompts to play your part.

(Say hello, and ask if they have a double room with a shower)
Per quante notti?
(Say for one night)
Sì, ma con bagno.
(Ask how much it is)
Novanta euro per notte.
(Ask if breakfast is included)
No, la colazione si paga a parte, cinque euro.
(Say fine, you'll take it)

linkup

key phrases

Ha una camera doppia?	**Do you have** a double room?
C'è l'ascensore?	**Is there** a lift?
Dov'è il ristorante?	**Where's** the restaurant?
Non c'è l'aria condizionata.	**There isn't any** air conditioning.
La doccia **non funziona**.	The shower **isn't working**.
Posso pagare con la carta di credito?	**Can I** pay by credit card?

ways of saying 'a'

In Italian, the word for 'a' changes depending on whether the noun it's referring to is masculine or feminine.

With masculine nouns use **un**:
un appartamento a flat   un balcone a balcony

With feminine nouns use **una**:
una camera doppia a double room   una notte one/a night

With masculine nouns that start with **s** + consonant, **z**, **ps**, **gn** or **y** (no need to worry, there aren't many!) use **uno**:
uno studio a studio

If the noun is feminine and starts with a vowel, use **un'**:
un'acqua minerale a mineral water

ways of saying 'the'

The word for 'the' changes, depending on the gender and number of the noun it refers to. With masculine words, when talking about one thing:

il for words starting with most consonants:

il bagno the bathroom   il letto the bed

l' for words starting with a vowel:

l'albergo hotel   l'ascensore the lift

lo for words starting with **z** or **s** + another consonant:

lo scaffale the bookshelf

With feminine words, when talking about one thing:

la for words starting with a consonant:

la colazione breakfast   la doccia the shower

l' for words starting with a vowel: l'acqua calda the hot water

When talking about more than one thing, 'the' is: i, gli or le. For more detail, see the Language Builder, p128. ·····⟩

negatives

As a general rule, to translate 'not', just insert non before the verb:

La doccia non funziona. The shower doesn't work.

La colazione non è inclusa. Breakfast isn't included.

availability

To find out if something is available, use c'è:

C'è l'aria condizionata? Is there air conditioning?

If you are referring to plural objects, use ci sono:

Ci sono due camere doppie? Do you have two double rooms?

Buying **Things**

opening hours

Shops are generally open Monday to Saturday 9am to 1pm and 4pm to 7.30pm, although some close for half a day during the week, usually on Monday mornings. Credit cards are commonly used, but don't be surprised if you are asked for your passport as proof of ID. Banks are open in the morning and for a few hours in the afternoon.

buying food

Most Italians shop in open-air markets for fresh produce. Prices are displayed and are non-negotiable. Otherwise, for everyday items, you can find a range of foods at **alimentari** (grocers') and small supermarkets. Most **alimentari** will also make up **panini** (rolls) for you. For delicacies and local specialities including salami, find a **salumeria** (delicatessen). Hypermarkets are usually located on the outskirts of large towns.

local goods

Lace The Venetian island of Burano is the centre for lace and embroidered linen, though it's on sale throughout the Venice area. Orvieto in Umbria is also a small-scale centre for **merletto** (lace).

Glass Ubiquitous in Venice, though often gaudy and kitsch. Shop around for the best deals. The island of Murano has many workshops open to visitors.

Masks Carnival masks achieve a rare refinement in Venice, while those in Sardinia are of a coarser, rustic style.

Ceramics Faenza, in Emilia-Romagna, is famed for its faience pottery. For decorative designs, head south to Vietri sul Mare, on the Amalfi coast, or Sicily's Caltagirone and Santo Stefano di Camastra.

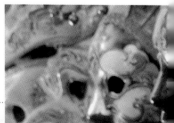

Jewellery Florence, especially the Ponte Vecchio, is a traditional centre for jewellers.

Woven rugs and baskets Sardinia specialises in these brightly coloured handicrafts.

Woodwork Orvieto is a major centre for wood-carved articles.

Puppets can be found in Palermo and Catania.

Shoes Good quality, well-designed leather footwear is good value in Milan and Florence.

Wine The best selection is at the local **enoteca** (wine shop), where you can often sample before buying. Look for the acronyms DOC or DOCG for the best quality wines, and the black rooster symbol for authentic Chianti.

Olive oil Puglia is one of Europe's biggest producers.

markets

Atmospheric and excellent for souvenirs, Italy's street markets are quintessential elements of daily life. The most animated include:

Rialto, Venice Still redolent of its medieval origins, now selling mainly fruit and vegetables.

San Lorenzo, Florence The street market has shoes, clothes and souvenirs. The nearby Mercato Centrale sells food.

Porta Portese, Rome A popular Sunday morning flea-market.

Piazza Vittorio, Rome A much smaller food market.

La Forcella, Naples A lively market that sells everything from live chickens to sunglasses.

Vucciria, Palermo A bustling, oriental-style market.

phrasemaker

general shopping phrases

you may say ...

Do you have ...	Ha ...	*a*
any milk?	del latte?	*del latte*
any stamps?	dei francobolli?	*de-ee frankobollee*
How much is it?	Quanto costa/viene?	*kwanto kosta/vyene*
How much are they?	Quanto costano/ vengono?	*kwanto kostano/ vengono*
this one, that one	questo/a, quello/a	*kwesto/a, kwello/a*
How much is it (altogether)?	Quant'è (in tutto)?	*kwante (een tootto)*
That's all, thank you.	Basta così, grazie.	*basta kozee gratsye*
Can I pay by credit card?	Posso pagare con la carta di credito?	*posso pagare kon la karta dee kredeeto*
I'm just looking, thank you.	Sto guardando, grazie.	*sto gwardando gratsye*

you may hear ...

Prego?/Desidera?/ Dica?	*prego/dezeedera/ deeka*	Can I help you?
No, mi dispiace.	*no mee deespyache*	I'm afraid not.
Quanto vuole?	*kwanto vwole*	How much would you like?
Quale?	*kwale*	Which one?
Altro?	*altro*	Anything else?
Ecco.	*ekko*	Here you are.
Allora, in tutto sono ... euro.	*allora een tootto sono ... e-ooro*	Well, that's ... euros altogether.

Buying **Things**

types of shops

baker's	il panificio/il forno	*eel paneefeecho/ eel forno*
bookshop	la libreria	*la leebreree*a
butcher's	la macelleria	*la machelleree*a
cake shop	la pasticceria	*la pasteecheree*a
chemist's	la farmacia	*la farmachee*a
clothes shop	il negozio di abbigliamento	*eel negotsyo dee abbeellyamento*
department store	il grande magazzino	*eel grande magadzeeno*
greengrocer's	il fruttivendolo	*eel frootteevendolo*
grocer's	il negozio di alimentari	*eel negotsyo dee aleementaree*
jeweller's	la gioielleria	*la joyelleree*a
newsagent's	il giornalaio/l'edicola	*eel jornalayo/ ledeekola*
photographic shop	il fotografo	*eel fotografo*
shoe shop	il negozio di scarpe/ calzature	*eel negotsyo dee skarpe/kaltsatoore*
stationer's	la cartoleria	*la kartoleree*a
tobacconist's	il tabacchino	*eel tabakeeno*
toy shop	il negozio di giocattoli	*eel negotsyo dee jokattolee*
travel agent's	l'agenzia di viaggi	*lajentseea dee vyajee*

quantities

you may say …

How much is it/ are they a kilo?	Quanto costa/ costano al chilo?	*kwanto kosta/ kostano al keelo*
I'll have a kilo of … apples tomatoes	Mi dà un chilo di … mele pomodori	*mee da oon keelo dee mele pomodoree*
half a kilo of … cherries grapes	mezzo chilo di … ciliegie uva	*medzo keelo dee cheelyeje oova*
100 grammes of parmesan	un etto di parmigiano	*oon etto dee parmeejano*
a litre of milk	un litro di latte	*oon leetro dee latte*
a bottle of …	una bottiglia di …	*oona botteelya dee*
a packet of …	un pacchetto di …	*oon paketto dee*
a slice/three slices of …	una fetta/tre fette di …	*oona fetta/tre fette dee*
a bit more/less	un po' di più/meno	*oon po dee pyoo/meno*
a tin (of tomatoes)	un barattolo (di pomodori)	*oon barattolo (dee pomodoree)*
can	una lattina	*oona latteena*

groceries

biscuits	i biscotti	*ee beeskotti*
butter	il burro	*eel boorro*
cheese	il formaggio	*eel formajo*
crisps	le patatine	*le patateene*
eggs	le uova	*le oo-ova*
ham/cured ham	il prosciutto cotto/ crudo	*eel proshootto kotto/ kroodo*
jam/marmalade	la marmellata	*la marmellata*
orange juice	il succo di frutta all'arancia	*eel sooko dee frootta all arancha*
washing-up liquid	il detersivo	*eel deterseevo*

(For cakes and pastries, see p76. For meat and fish, see Menu Reader, p93.)

Buying **Things**

fruit & vegetables

apples	le mele	*le mele*
apricots	le albicocche	*le albee**kokke***
aubergines	le melanzane	*le melan**tsane***
bananas	le banane	*le ba**nane***
basil	il basilico	*eel ba**zee**leeko*
carrots	le carote	*le ka**ro**te*
figs	i fichi	*ee **fee**kee*
French beans	i fagiolini	*ee fajo**lee**nee*
garlic	l'aglio	*lalyo*
lemons	i limoni	*ee lee**mo**nee*
lettuce	la lattuga	*la lat**too**ga*
melon	il melone	*eel me**lone***
mushrooms	i funghi	*ee **foon**gee*
oranges	le arance	*le a**ranche***
peaches	le pesche	*le **pes**ke*
pears	le pere	*le **pere***
pineapple	l'ananas	*lananas*
plums	le prugne	*le **proon**ye*
potatoes	le patate	*le pa**tate***
raspberries	i lamponi	*ee lam**po**nee*
spinach	gli spinaci	*lyee spee**na**chee*
strawberries	le fragole	*le **fra**gole*
tomatoes	i pomodori	*ee pomo**do**ree*
watermelon	il cocomero	*eel ko**ko**mero*

check out 1

You want to buy some fresh fruit and vegetables.

○ Dica.
  deeka

- Mezzo chilo di ciliegie e un chilo di pomodori, per per favore.
  medzo keelo dee cheelyeje e oon keelo dee pomodoree per favore

○ Tre euro e cinquanta le ciliegie, due e ottanta i pomodori. Altro?
  tre e-ooro e cheenkwanta le cheelyeje doo-e e ottanta ee pomodoree. altro

- Ha dell'uva?
  a dell'oova

○ Sì, ecco.
  see ekko

- Quanto costa al chilo?
  kwanto kosta al keelo

○ Tre e venti.
  tre e ventee

- Mezzo chilo, per favore.
  medzo keelo per favore

○ Altro?
  altro

- Basta così, grazie. Quant'è?
  basta kozee gratsye. kwante

Q What is the first fruit you ask for?
You buy a kilo of grapes: true or false?

Buying **Things**

buying clothes & shoes

you may say...

I'm just looking, thank you.	Sto guardando, grazie.	*sto gwardando gratsye*
I'd like ...	Vorrei ...	*vorre-ee*
a shirt.	una camicia.	*oona kameecha*
a pair of trousers.	un paio di pantaloni.	*oon piyo dee pantalonee*
I'm a ...	Ho ...	*o*
size 46. (clothes)	la taglia 46.	*la talya kwarantase-ee*
size 38. (shoes)	il numero 38.	*eel noomero trentotto*
Can I try it on?	Posso provarlo/la?	*posso provarlo/la*
Can I try them on?	Posso provarli/le?	*posso provarlee/le*
It's too ...	È troppo ...	*e troppo*
big.	grande.	*grande*
small.	piccolo/a.	*peekkolo/a*
They're too ...	Sono troppo ...	*sono troppo*
big.	grandi.	*grandee*
small.	piccoli/e.	*peekkolee/e*
Do you have a smaller size? (for clothes/for shoes)	Ha la taglia più piccola/il numero più piccolo?	*a la talya pyoo peekkola/eel noomero pyoo peekkolo*
Do you have anything cheaper?	Ha qualcosa di più economico?	*a kwalkoza dee pyoo ekonomeeko*
Do you have the same in ...	Ha lo stesso modello in ...	*a lo stesso modello een*
yellow?	giallo?	*jallo*
cotton?	cotone?	*kotone*
silk?	seta?	*seta*
wool?	lana?	*lana*
linen?	lino?	*leeno*
I (don't) like ...	(Non) Mi ...	*(non) mee*
it.	piace.	*pyache*
them.	piacciono.	*pyachono*

(For help on the different words for 'it' and 'them', see the Language Builder, p133.)

I'll take it.	Lo/La prendo.	*lo/la **prendo***
I'll take them.	Li/Le prendo.	*lee/le **prendo***
I'll think about it.	Ci penso.	*chee **pen**so*
Can I have a discount?	Mi fa uno sconto?	*mee fa **oo**no **sko**nto*

Che ...	*ke*	What size?
taglia?	***ta**lya*	(for clothes)
numero?	***noo**mero*	(for shoes)
Di che colore?	*dee ke ko**lo**re*	What colour?
Il camerino è là in fondo.	*eel kame**ree**no e la een **fon**do*	The changing room is there at the back.
Come ...	***ko**me*	How ...
va?	*va*	does it fit?
vanno?	***van**no*	do they fit?

colours

black	nero/a	***ne**ro/a*
blue	blu	*blu*
brown	marrone	*mar**ro**ne*
green	verde	***ver**de*
grey	grigio/a	***gree**jo/a*
orange	arancio/a	*a**ran**cho/a*
pink	rosa	***ro**za*
purple	viola	***vyo**la*
red	rosso/a	***ro**sso/a*
white	bianco/a	***bya**nko/a*
yellow	giallo/a	***ja**llo/a*

Buying **Things**

clothes & accessories

bag	la borsetta	*la borsetta*
belt	la cintura	*la cheentoora*
coat	il cappotto	*eel kappotto*
gloves	i guanti	*ee gwantee*
hat	il cappello	*eel kappello*
jacket	la giacca	*la jakka*
raincoat	l'impermeabile (m)	*leemperme-abeele*
scarf	la sciarpa	*la sharpa*
shirt/blouse	la camicia	*la kameecha*
shoes	le scarpe	*le skarpe*
skirt	la gonna	*la gonna*
socks	i calzini	*ee kalzeenee*
sunglasses	gli occhiali da sole	*lyee okyalee da sole*
sweater	il maglione	*eel malyone*
swimming costume/ trunks	il costume da bagno	*eel kostoome da banyo*
T-shirt	la maglietta	*la malyetta*
tie	la cravatta	*la kravatta*
tights	il collant	*eel kollant*
trousers	i pantaloni	*ee pantalonee*
watch	l'orologio (m)	*lorolojo*

department store

you may say...

Where is the ... department?	Dov'è il reparto ...	*dove eel reparto*
food	alimentari?	*aleementaree*
toy	giochi?	*jokee*
Is there a lift?	C'è l'ascensore?	*che lashensore*

you may hear...

al pianterreno	*al pyanterreno*	on the ground floor
al primo/secondo piano	*al preemo/sekondo pyano*	on the first/second floor
nel seminterrato	*nel semeenterrato*	in the basement

check out 2

In a market, you pick out some shoes you like.

○ Scusi, quanto costano?
skoozee kwanto kostano

- Vengono quarantanove. Che numero?
vengono kwarantanove. ke noomero

○ Trentotto.
trentotto

- Ecco. Come vanno?
ekko. kome vanno

○ Bene, ma ... ha qualcosa di più economico, o mi
fa uno sconto?
*bene ma a kwalkoza dee pyoo ekonomiko o mee
fa oono skonto*

- No, no, mi dispiace.
no no mee deespyache

○ Allora ... ci penso.
allora chee penso

- Va bene, allora, quarantacinque.
va bene allora kwarantacheenkwe

○ Le prendo.
le prendo

Q How much do the shoes cost originally?
What is the reduced price?

Buying **Things**

getting photos developed

Can you develop this film?	Mi sviluppa questo rullino?	mee svee**loo**ppa kwe**sto** rool**lee**no
Can I have my digital images printed?	Posso stampare queste immagini digitali?	po**sso** stam**pa**re kwe**ste** eemma**jee**nee deejee**ta**lee
Can I print from this memory card?	Posso stampare da questa scheda (di memoria)?	po**sso** stam**pa**re da kwesta **ske**da (dee me**mo**rya)
When will it be ready?	Quando sarà pronto?	kwando sara **pron**to
a packet of batteries	una confezione di pile	oona konfe**tsyo**ne dee **pee**le
a disposable camera	una macchina usa e getta	oona makeena **oo**za e jetta
matt/gloss photos	foto opache/lucide	foto o**pa**ke/loo**chee**de
camera	la macchina fotografica	la makeena foto**gra**feeka

Quale formato vuole?	kwale for**ma**to vwole	What size do you want your prints?
questo pomeriggio	kwesto pome**ree**jo	this afternoon
domani mattina	do**ma**nee mat**tee**na	tomorrow morning
fra ...	fra	in ...
un'ora	oon **o**ra	an hour
tre ore	tre **o**re	three hours

at the post office

How much is a stamp for ...	Quanto costa un francobollo per ...	kwanto kosta oon frankobollo per
Great Britain?	la Gran Bretagna?	la gran bretanya
the United States?	gli Stati Uniti?	lee statee ooneetee
Four stamps, please.	Quattro francobolli, per favore.	kwattro frankobollee per favore
a stamp for a postcard	un francobollo da cartolina	oon frankobollo da kartoleena
a €5 telephone card	una carta telefonica da cinque euro	oona karta telefoneeka da cheenkwee-ooro
I'd like to send this to England.	Vorrei spedire questo/a in Inghilterra.	vorre-ee spedeere kwesto/a een eengeelterra

at the newsagent's

Do you have ...	Ha ...	a
English newspapers?	dei giornali inglesi?	de-ee jornalee eenglezee
American magazines?	delle riviste americane?	delle reeveeste amereekane
I'd like ...	Vorrei ...	vorre-ee
a guidebook.	una guida.	oona gweeda
a map of the city.	una piantina della città.	oona pyanteena della cheetta
a pack of cigarettes.	un pacchetto di sigarette.	oon paketto dee seegarette
some matches.	dei fiammiferi.	de-ee fyammeeferee
a postcard.	una cartolina.	oona kartoleena

check out 3

You need to buy stamps, a phone card and something to read.

- ○ Prego?
  prego

- − Quanto costa un francobollo per la Gran Bretagna?
  kwanto kosta oon frankobollo per la gran bretanya

- ○ Costa sessantacinque centesimi.
  kosta sessantacheenkwee chentezeemee

- − Vorrei due francobolli e una carta telefonica da venti euro.
  vorre-ee doo-e frankobollee e oona karta telefoneeka da ventee e-ooro

- ○ Altro?
  altro

- − Prendo un giornale.
  prendo oon jornale

- ○ Allora, in tutto sono ventitré euro.
  allora een tootto sono venteetre e-ooro

Q How many stamps do you want?
How much do you pay?

sound check

g is pronounced differently, depending on the vowel that follows it.

g + **e** or **i** sounds like the 'j' in 'jeans':

gelato *jelato*   formaggio *formajjo*

g + **a**, **o** or **u** sounds like 'g' in 'go':

gamba *gamba*   gola *gola*

ragù *ragoo*

g + **h** is also like 'g' in 'go':

inghilterra *eengeelterra*

Practise on these words:

buongiorno *bwonjorno*   gentile *jenteele*

ghiaccio *gyacho*   ragazza *ragatsa*

try it out

mind the gap

Use the phrases a-d to complete the following sentences. They're all things you might say when shopping.

1   Una cartolina e un _____ per l'Inghilterra.
2   Una _____ per la macchina fotografica.
3   Posso pagare con la _____?
4   Una _____ per telefonare.

a   carta telefonica
b   carta di credito
c   scheda di memoria
d   francobollo

colouring in

Can you name all of these colours in Italian?
The colour of ...

1 a stop light
2 grass
3 milk
4 a canary
5 the sea
6 an orange
7 a plum
8 coal

as if you were there

You are at a market and spot some nice sunglasses
– occhiali da sole. Follow the prompts to play your part.

(Point to a pair of sunglasses and ask how much they are)
Quarantotto euro.

(Ask if he has anything cheaper)
Ecco a lei venticinque.

(Tell him you don't like them)
Gli occhiali da quarantotto sono firmati.

(He says the €48 pair are designer: ask for a discount)
Mi dispiace, quarantotto.

(Say you'll think about it and thank him)
Va bene, quarantacinque.

linkup

key phrases

Dov'è il reparto musicale?	**Where's** the music department?
Mi dà due chili di …	**I'll have** two kilos of …
Quanto costa questa gonna?	**How much is** this skirt?
Quanto costano i biscotti?	**How much are** the biscuits?
Ha la taglia più piccolo?	**Do you have** a smaller size?
Vorrei un francobollo per l'Inghilterra.	**I'd like** a stamp for England.
Mi piace questo vaso.	**I like** this vase.

more than one

In the plural, a masculine noun ending in **-o**, e.g. un francobollo, changes to **-i**:
Vorrei tre francobolli. I'd like three stamps.

A feminine noun ending in **-a**, e.g. una guida, changes to **-e**:
Due guide, per favore. Two guides, please.

Nouns ending in **-e**, irrespective of their gender, change to **-i** in the plural:
Un giornale, per favore. A newspaper, please.
Due giornali, per favore. Two newspapers, please.

adjectives

Adjectives (words used to describe things and people) have different endings depending on whether the thing they are referring to is masculine or feminine. The usual pattern is **-o** for masculine adjectives and **-a** for feminine adjectives:
un pomodoro ross**o** a red tomato
una fragola ross**a** a red strawberry

But adjectives ending in **-e** remain the same, whatever the gender of the thing they refer to:
un vestito verd**e** a green dress
una borsa verd**e** a green bag

Notice that most adjectives come after the noun in Italian.
una borsa **grande** ed **elegante** a large and elegant bag

When talking about more than one thing, adjectives ending in **-a** change to **-e**:
una fragola ross**a** a red strawberry
due fragole ross**e** two red strawberries

Adjectives ending **-o** or **-e** change to **-i** in the plural:
questo vaso piccol**o** this small vase
questi vasi piccol**i** these small vases
questo cappello grand**e** this large hat
questi cappelli grand**i** these large hats

comparatives

If you want to ask for a bigger or smaller size you use
più or meno – more or less – and a relevant adjective.
For example:
Ha la taglia più grande? Do you have a bigger size? (literally, Do you have the size more big?)
Ha la taglia più piccola? Do you have a smaller size? (literally, Do you have the size more small?)

Café **Life**

Cafés and bars are an important part of the Italian lifestyle, busy from early morning to late at night. They serve a wide variety of alcohol and hot drinks, and most also serve snacks, usually sandwiches and pastries. There are no age restrictions.

Bars are a good place to have breakfast; Italians normally stand at a bar and gulp their cappuccino or **caffè espresso** (small black coffee) and eat a **cornetto** (croissant). If you are served at the table, you are charged 50–100% more.

If you simply order **caffè** (coffee), you'll get a small, strong espresso. For something more similar to what you are used to at home, ask for **caffè americano**. Cappuccino is mostly a breakfast drink. You could also try **caffè macchiato** (coffee with a little milk), **latte macchiato** (glass of milk with a little coffee), or **caffè corretto** (espresso with schnapps).

An evening meal may be preceded by an aperitif at a bar, and followed by a coffee or homemade ice cream at a gelateria (ice cream parlour). You can also try regional sweets in a **pasticceria** (cake shop).

Beer is usually served in smaller measures than in the UK and tends to be relatively expensive. Most bars sell **birra alla spina** (draught beer), and have a large selection of imported bottled beers. Wine is much cheaper. An alternative to beer and wine is the aromatic Campari, or a refreshing Bellini (sparkling wine and peach juice). After your meal, try a strong liqueur, such as the very sweet walnut **nocino** and the lemony **limoncello**.

phrasemaker

asking what there is
you may say ...

Do you have any ...	Ha dei ...	a de-ee
sandwiches?	tramezzini?	tramedzeenee
rolls?	panini?	paneenee
What ... do you have?	Che ... ha?	ke ... a
rolls	panini	paneenee
cakes	paste	paste
soft drinks	bibite	beebeete

you may hear ...

Prego?/Desidera?	prego/dezeedera	What would you like?
Mi dispiace, ...	mee deespyache	Sorry, ...
è finito/a.	e feeneeto/a	we've run out of it.
sono finiti/e.	sono feeneetee/e	we've run out of them.

soft drinks

coke	una coca-cola	oona koka-kola
... juice	un succo di ...	oon sookko dee
fruit	frutta	frootta
grapefruit	pompelmo	pompelmo
peach	pesca	peska
pear	pera	pera
freshly squeezed orange juice	una spremuta d'arancia	oona spremoota darancha
iced tea	un tè freddo	oon te freddo
lemonade	una limonata	oona leemonata
milk	un latte	oon latte
milkshake	un frullato	oon froollato
mineral water ...	un'acqua minerale ...	oon akkwa meenerale
still	naturale	natoorale
fizzy	gassata	gassata
tonic	un'acqua tonica	oon akkwa toneeka

check out 1

You are looking for a sandwich for your lunch.

- ○ Ha dei tramezzini?
  a de-ee tramedzeenee

- — Mi dispiace, solo panini: i tramezzini sono finiti.
  mee deespyache solo paneenee: ee tramedzeenee sono feeneetee

- ○ Che panini ha?
  ke paneenee a

- — Al formaggio, al prosciutto, al salame ...
  al formajjo al proshootto al salame

- ○ Un panino al formaggio e due birre.
  oon paneeno al formajjo e doo-e beerre

- — Ecco a lei. Allora il panino quattro euro e le birre sei.
  ekko a le-ee. allora eel paneeno kwattro e-ooro e le beerre se-ee.

Q There are only rolls left: true or false?
A beer costs €2.50: true or false?

alcoholic drinks

(draft) beer	una birra (alla spina)	*oona beerra (alla speena)*
... wine	un vino ...	*oon veeno*
white	bianco	*byanko*
red	rosso	*rosso*
rosé	rosato	*rozato*
dry	secco	*sekko*
sparkling	spumante	*spoomante*
sweet	dolce	*dolche*
brandy	un cognac	*oon konyak*
whisky	un whisky	*oon weeskee*
gin (and tonic)	un gin (tonic)	*oon jeen (toneek)*

hot drinks

un caffè	*oon kaffe*	coffee
un caffè corretto	*oon kafe korretto*	coffee with a liqueur such as grappa or cognac
un caffè lungo	*oon kaffe loongo*	weaker black coffee, served in a long glass
un cappuccino	*oon kappoocheeno*	cappuccino
un caffè macchiato	*oon kaffe makkyato*	coffee with just a little milk
una cioccolata	*oona chokkolata*	hot chocolate
un latte macchiato	*oon latte makkyato*	milk with a little coffee
un tè ...	*oon te*	tea ...
al latte	*al latte*	with milk
al limone	*al leemone*	with lemon
una tisana	*oona teezana*	herbal tea
con/senza ...	*kon/sentsa*	with/without ...
panna	*panna*	cream
zucchero	*zookkero*	sugar

ordering

I'll have ..., please.	Vorrei ..., per favore.	*vorre-ee ... per favore*
a cheese roll	un panino al formaggio	*oon paneeno al formajjo*
a small pizza	una pizzetta	*oona peetsetta*
a white coffee	un caffè macchiato	*oon kafe makkyato*
a hot chocolate	una cioccolata	*oona chokkolata*
with a slice of lemon	con una fetta di limone	*kon oona fetta dee leemone*
with/without ice	con/senza ghiaccio	*kon/sentsa gyacho*
this one	questo/a	*kwestola*
that one	quello/a	*kwellola*

Quale?	*kwale*	Which one?
Ecco a lei.	*ekko a le-ee*	Here you are.
Si serva pure.	*see serva poore*	Help yourself./It's self-service.
Con ...	*kon ...*	With ...
panna?	*panna*	cream?
ghiaccio?	*gyacho*	ice?
limone?	*leemone*	lemon?
Qualcosa da bere?	*kwalkoza da bere*	Something to drink?
Gassata o naturale?	*gassata o natoorale*	Fizzy or still?
In cono o coppetta?	*een kono o koppetta*	In a cone or a tub?
Che gusto?	*ke goosto*	Which flavour (of ice cream)?
Deve fare lo scontrino alla cassa.	*deve fare lo skontreeno alla kassa*	You need to get a receipt first at the till.

Café **Life**

check out 2

In a busy café, you order hot drinks and croissants for you and your friend.

○ Un cappuccino, una cioccolata calda e due cornetti, per favore.
oon kappoocheeno oona chokkolata kalda e doo-e kornettee per favore

- La cioccolata con panna?
la chokkolata kon panna

○ No, senza.
no sentsa

- Per i cornetti si serva pure.
per ee kornettee see serva poore

○ Grazie.
gratsye.

Q Do you want cream with the hot chocolate?
You can help yourself to the croissants: true or false?

snacks

small pizza	la pizzetta	*la peetsetta*
slice of pizza ...	una fetta di pizza ...	*oona fetta dee peetsa*
with cheese	al formaggio	*al formajjo*
with mushrooms	ai funghi	*a-ee foongee*
bread roll ...	il panino ...	*eel paneeno*
with Parma ham	al prosciutto crudo	*al proshootto kroodo*
with salami	al salame	*al salame*
sandwich ...	il tramezzino ...	*eel tramedzeeno*
with cooked ham	al prosciutto cotto	*al proshootto kotto*
with tuna and tomatoes	al tonno e pomodoro	*al tonno e pomodoro*

cakes & pastries

una bombolone	*oona bombolone*	doughnut
una brioche	*oona breeosh*	brioche
cannoli	*kannolee*	tube-shaped shells of fried pasta with creamy filling
cassata	*kassata*	Sicilian candied fruit cake with liqueur chocolate filling
un cornetto ...	*oon kornetto*	croissant ...
alla crema	*alla krema*	with cream
alla marmellata	*alla marmellata*	with jam
pandoro	*pandoro*	Christmas sweet yeast bread dusted with vanilla
panettone	*panettone*	Christmas bread cake with candied fruit
senza uvetta	*sentsa oovetta*	without raisins
sfogliatella	*sfolyatella*	shell-shaped flaky pastry filled with sweet ricotta cheese

containers

cone	il cono	*eel kono*
carafe	la caraffa	*la karaffa*
glass	il bicchiere	*eel beekkyere*
scoop	la pallina	*la paleena*
tub	la coppetta	*la koppetta*

Café **Life**

ice cream

you may say ...

I'll have ...	Vorrei ...	*vorre-ee*
a lemon ice cream.	un gelato al limone.	*oon jelato al leemone*
two ice creams.	due gelati.	*doo-e jelatee*
bilberry	ai mirtilli	*ayee meerteellee*
chocolate	al cioccolato	*al chokkolato*
chocolate chip	alla stracciatella	*alla strachatella*
coconut	al cocco	*al kokko*
creamy vanilla	al fiordilatte	*al fyordeelatte*
fruits of the forest	ai frutti di bosco	*ayee froottee dee bosko*
hazelnut	alla nocciola	*alla nochola*
pistachio	al pistacchio	*al peestakkyo*
raspberry	al lampone	*al lampone*
strawberry	alla fragola	*alla fragola*
vanilla	alla crema	*alla krema*

check out 3

Out sightseeing with your family, you stop for a refreshing ice cream.

○ Tre gelati da due e uno da due e cinquanta, per favore.
tre jelatee da doo-e e oono da doo-e e cheenkwanta per favore

- In cono o in coppetta?
een kono o een koppetta

○ In cono.
een kono.

- Che gusto?
ke goosto

○ Due al limone e due alla stracciatella e nocciola.
doo-e al leemone e doo-e alla strachatella e nocchola

Q You pay with a €10 note: how much change do you get?

other useful phrases

you may say ...

How much is it (altogether)?	Quant'è (in tutto)?	*kwante (een tootto)*	
Is there a telephone?	C'è il telefono?	*che eel telefono*	
Where are the toilets?	Dove sono le toilette?	*dove sono le toylette*	
Here you are.	Ecco.	*ekko*	

you may hear ...

| In tutto è cinque euro. | *een tooto e cheenkwe e-ooro* | It's €5 in total. |
| Ce n'è una/uno lì dietro. | *che ne oona/oono lee dyetro* | There's one back there. |

sound check

The pronunciation of **s** changes depending on the letters around it.

s between two vowels sounds like the 's' in 'rose':

naso *nazo*   casa *caza*

s + anything else sounds like the 's' in 'state':

estate *estate*   posso *posso*

Practise on these words:

qualcosa *kwalkoza*   scusi *skoozee*
gassata *gassata*   rosso *rosso*

try it out

match it up
Put together the parts of words below to find five flavours of ice cream.

CRE   FRA   NOC   CO   PISTAC

CIOLA   MA   CCO   CHIO   GOLA

question time
Can you match the questions on the left to the answers on the right? They're all things you might say or hear in a café.

1 Quale?   a Una brioche, per favore.
2 Che gusto?   b Cinque euro e quindici.
3 Prego?   c Sì, un Martini, per favore.
4 Quant'è?   d Questa.
5 Qualcosa da bere?   e Stracciatella.

as if you were there
You are at a gelateria in Rome, choosing ice cream. Follow the prompts to play your part.

Prego?
(Ask what flavours they have)
Limone, stracciatella, fragola, nocciola …
(Say you'd like one strawberry and one lemon ice cream)
In cono o in coppetta?
(Say you'd like them in a tub)
Va bene. Sei euro in tutto.
(Give him the money and thank him)

linkup

Ha dei gelati?	**Have you got** any ice creams?
Ha del latte?	**Have you got** any milk?
Che panini **ha**?	**What** rolls **do you have**?
Prendo una birra.	**I'll have** a beer.
Vorrei un caffè, per favore.	**I'd like** a black coffee, please.

asking for things

The simplest way to ask for things is to state the item you want and add 'please':

Una birra, per favore. A beer, please.

You can also use:

Vorrei un panino. I'd like a roll.

Or:

Prendo une pizza.

Mi dà una brioche?

Mi fa un caffè americano?

Which all mean 'I'll have ...'.

You don't need to use per favore with mi fa and mi dà as they are already polite expressions.

some/any

The expression for 'some/any' changes according to whether the noun you are referring to is masculine or feminine, singular or plural.

For example, if you are asking for one thing, which happens to be masculine, you say:

Ha **del** latte? Have you got any milk?

For more than one masculine thing:

Ha **dei** cornetti alla cioccolata? Have you got any chocolate croissants?

The same happens for feminine nouns:

Ha **della** pizza? Have you got any pizza? (feminine singular)

Ha **delle** bibite fresche? Have you got any cold drinks? (feminine plural)

If in doubt about how to use 'any' or 'some' then you can leave them out and still be understood. For example, although not strictly correct, ha fragole? will be understood by Italian native speakers.

For more on 'some' and 'any', see the Language Builder, p134. ⋯⋯⟩

Eating **Out**

meals

Lunch takes place from noon to 2pm, and varies from a quick **tramezzino** (sandwich) or **panino** (roll) to a restaurant affair. The evening meal is eaten from about 8pm to 11pm.

Vegetarians can choose from a wide range of pasta and vegetable sauces (though some may contain meat stock – check with the waiter).

Italians place a high emphasis on service and will try to accommodate special requests, like allergies and children's portions. A **coperto** (cover charge) per person will be added to the bill for a sit-down meal.

where to eat

Tavola calda Offers fast-food Italian-style: pre-cooked pasta, pizzas and meat dishes. Licenced.

Pizzeria Serves pizzas, beers and sometimes other dishes. The best have a **forno a legna** (wood-fired oven).

Trattoria Informal, often family-run establishment with local wine and dishes. Not all have a written menu – ask for recommendations.

Osteria Specialises in country fare, and ranges from a down-to-earth tavern to a chic restaurant.

Ristorante More formal and expensive restaurant with a more extensive menu.

Smoking in restaurants, bars and clubs is banned unless they have an **area fumatori** (smoking area).

courses

Antipasto (starter) usually includes cold meats, and seafood and vegetable dishes. **Antipasti assortiti** (a selection of starters) can be brought to your table to choose from.

Primo (first main dish) will be a type of pasta, polenta or risotto (rice dish).

Secondo (second main dish) is the fish or meat course. Note that fish is usually priced by weight, and restaurants must specify if it is **surgelato** (frozen).

Contorno (side dish) is usually either a salad or vegetables.

Dolce (dessert) will be a choice of fruit, ice cream or cake.

what to try

The food on offer in an Italian restaurant varies enormously according to the region. Pasta is popular everywhere, while polenta is a favourite starter in Northern Italy. Lamb and veal are often on menus, but you will also find rabbit, game and wild boar in central Italy, pork as a staple in the Veneto and Calabria, and horsemeat in Sardinia. Some regional specialities to look out for include:

Emilia-Romagna Prosciutto (ham), parmigiano (parmesan cheese), tortellini, Lambrusco.

Lazio Gnocchi (potato dumplings), saltimbocca alla romana (rolled veal slices filled with cheese and ham), Frascati.

Liguria Lasagne/trenette al pesto (ribbon pasta with a basil, garlic, pine nuts and parmesan sauce).

Lombardy Risotto alla milanese (with saffron), cotoletta alla milanese (veal in breadcrumbs), gorgonzola blue cheese, osso buco (veal shank in wine).

Piedmont Barolo, Barbera wines.

Naples Spaghetti alle vongole (clams), pizza margherita.

Sardinia Carta di musica (poppadom-like bread), Cannonau wine, Mirto (liqueur made with myrtle berries).

Sicily Arancini (filled rice balls), caponata (Mediterranean sauce), involtini (stuffed aubergine rolls), pescespada (swordfish), Marsala.

Tuscany Bruschetta (garlic bread made with olive oil), triglie alla livornese (red mullet), bistecca alla fiorentina (T-bone steak), cinghiale (wild boar), panforte (sticky cake), Chianti.

Umbria Porcini (wild mushroooms), tartufo (truffle).

Venice Risi e bisi (rice with cured meat and peas), fegato alla veneziana (liver in onion sauce), zuppa di cozze (mussel soup), risotto alle seppie (squid risotto), Merlot, Tocai, Bardolino.

phrasemaker

finding somewhere to eat

you may say ...

Is there a good restaurant nearby?	C'è un buon ristorante qui vicino?	*che oon bwon reestorante kwee veecheeno*
Can you recommend a good Chinese restaurant?	Mi può consigliare un buon ristorante cinese?	*mee pwo konseelyare oon bwon reestorante cheeneze*
I'd like to book a table for ...	Vorrei riservare un tavolo per ...	*vorre-ee reezervare oon tavolo per*
tomorrow night.	domani sera.	*domanee sera*
this evening at 8.30pm.	stasera alle otto e mezza.	*stasera alle otto e medza*
four people.	quattro persone.	*kwattro persone*
A table for two.	Un tavolo per due.	*oon tavolo per doo-e*
I have a reservation for ...	Ho prenotato per ...	*o prenotato per*

you may hear ...

Mi dispiace, stasera siamo pieni.	*mee deespyache stasera syamo pyenee*	Sorry, we're full tonight.
Ritorni fra mezz'ora.	*reetornee fra medzora*	Come back in about half an hour.

Eating **Out**

asking about the menu

Can I have the menu, please?	Mi porta il menù?	*mee porta eel menoo*
What is …?	Che cos'è …?	*ke koze*
What's the local speciality?	Qual'è la specialità locale?	*kwale la spechaleeta lokale*
What do you recommend?	Che cosa consiglia?	*ke koza konseelya*
Do you have …	Ha …	*a*
seafood?	dei frutti di mare?	*de-ee froottee dee mare*
risotto?	del risotto?	*del reezotto*
Is it …	È …	*e*
strong?	forte?	*forte*
spicy?	piccante?	*peekkante*
Is … included?	È incluso …	*e eenkloozo eel*
bread	il pane?	*pane*
the cover charge	il coperto?	*koperto*

È …	*e*	It's …
un pesce.	*oon peshe*	a fish.
una varietà di funghi.	*oona varee-eta dee foongee*	a type of mushroom.
un sugo.	*oon soogo*	a (pasta) sauce.
una salsa.	*oona salsa*	a sauce/gravy.
Oggi abbiamo …	*ojjee abbyamo*	Today we have …
(Non) è incluso.	*(non) e eenkloozo*	It's (not) included.
Si paga a parte.	*see paga a parte*	It's extra.
Mi dispiace, … è finito/a.	*mee deespyache … e feeneetola*	Sorry, we haven't got any … left.

ordering

I'd like the set menu, please.	Vorrei il menù a prezzo fisso, per favore.	*vorre-ee eel menoo a pretso feesso per favore.*

I'll have ...	Prendo/Per me ...	*prendo/per me*
To drink ...	Da bere ...	*da bere*
As a ...	Come ...	*kome*
first course	primo	*preemo*
second course	secondo	*sekondo*
side dish	contorno	*kontorno*
dessert	dessert/dolce	*desser/dolche*
No ... for me.	Niente ... per me.	*nyente ... per me*
starter	antipasto	*anteepasto*
coffee	caffè	*kaffe*
rare/medium/ well done	al sangue/a puntino/ ben cotta	*al sangwe/ a poonteeno/ben kotta*
without ...	senza ...	*sentsa*
onions	cipolle	*cheepolle*

you may hear ...

Pronti per ordinare?	*prontee per ordeenare*	Are you ready to order?
(Che) cosa prende/ prendono?	*(ke) koza prende/ prendono*	What would you like?
Come la/lo vuole?	*kome (la/lo) vwole*	How do you want it?
Vuole il dessert?	*vwole eel desser*	Would you like a dessert?

Eating **Out**

check out 1

At a restaurant, you choose a menu and order something to drink.

○ Vorrei il menù a prezzo fisso.
  vorre-ee eel menoo a pretso feesso

- Ecco a lei. Da bere cosa prendono?
  ekko a le-ee. da bere koza prendono

○ Da bere, una birra e una limonata, per favore.
  Scusi, è incluso il pane?
  da bere oona beerra e oona leemonata per favore.
  scoozee e eenkloozo eel pane

- No, si paga a parte.
  no, see paga a parte

Q Bread is not included in the price: true or false?

eating preferences
you may say ...

Does it contain ...	Contiene/C'è ...	*kontyene/che*
meat?	carne?	*karne*
meat stock?	brodo di carne?	*brodo dee karne*
wheat?	glutine?	*glooteene*
garlic?	aglio?	*alyo*
I'm allergic to ...	Sono allergico/a ...	*sono allerjeeko/a*
nuts.	alle arachidi e noci.	*alle arakeedee e nochee*
seafood.	ai frutti di mare.	*a-ee frootee dee mare*
I'm vegetarian.	Sono vegetariano/a.	*sono vejetaryano/a*
I'm vegan.	Non mangio latticini, carne e uova.	*non manjo latteechee-nee karne e oo-ova*
I can't eat ...	Non posso mangiare ...	*non posso manjare*
dairy products.	latticini.	*latteecheenee*

87

drinks

(See p71 and p73 for more drinks.)

you may say ...

Can I have ... please?	Posso avere ... per favor?	*posso avere ... per favore*
the drinks menu	la lista delle bevande	*la lista delle bevande*
the wine list	la lista dei vini	*la lista de-ee veenee*
a bottle/carafe of ...	una bottiglia/caraffa di ...	*oona botteelya/karaffa dee*
half a bottle of ...	mezza bottiglia di ...	*medza botteelya dee*
house wine	vino della casa	*veeno della kaza*
a beer	una birra	*oona beerra*
sparkling/still	gassata/naturale	*gassata/natoorale*
mineral water	acqua minerale	*akwa meenerale*
tap water	acqua del rubinetto	*akwa del roobeenetto*

check out 2

You've booked a table for a meal on your last evening in Italy.

○ Buonasera. Ho prenotato per due, Florio.
bwonasera. o prenotato per doo-e floryo

- Sì, da questa parte, prego. Ecco il menù.
see da kwesta parte prego. ekko eel menoo

(later)

- Pronti per ordinare?
prontee per ordeenare

○ Sì, grazie, da bere una bottiglia di acqua minerale gassata e una bottiglia di vino bianco.
see gratsye da bere oona botteelya dee akkwa meenerale gassata e oona botteelya dee veeno byanko

Q What do you order to drink?

Eating **Out**

during the meal

Excuse me!/Waiter!	Scusi!/Cameriere!	*skoozee/kameryere*
I didn't order any ...	Non ho ordinato ...	*non o ordeenato*
More bread, please.	Mi porta ancora un po' di pane, per favore?	*me porta ankora un po dee pane per favore*
Another bottle of ...	Un'altra bottiglia di ...	*oon altra botteelya dee e*
It's ...	È ...	
delicious.	squisito.	*skweezeeto*
very good.	molto buono.	*molto bwono*
cold.	freddo.	*freddo*
raw.	crudo.	*kroodo*
burnt.	bruciato.	*broochato*

Per chi è il risotto di pesce?	*per kee e eel reezotto dee peshe*	Who is the fish risotto for?
Tutto bene?	*tootto bene*	Is everything all right?
Altro?	*altro*	Anything else?
Buon appetito!	*bwon appeteeto*	Enjoy your meal!

on your table

coffee cup	la tazzina	*la tatseena*
fork	la forchetta	*la forketta*
glass	il bicchiere	*eel beekkyere*
knife	il coltello	*eel koltello*
napkin	il tovagliolo	*eel tovalyolo*
oil/vinegar	l'olio/l'aceto	*lolyo/lacheto*
plate	il piatto	*eel pyatto*
salt/pepper	il sale/il pepe	*eel sale/eel pepe*
spoon/teaspoon	il cucchiaio/ il cucchiaino	*eel kookya-yo/ eel kookya-eeno*
tablecloth	la tovaglia	*la tovalya*

paying
you may say ...

The bill, please.	Mi porta il conto, per favore?	*me porta eel konto per favore*
Do you take credit cards?	Accettate carte di credito?	*achetate karte dee kredeeto*
There is a mistake, I think.	C'è un errore, credo.	*che oon errore kredo.*
We didn't have any ... beer.	Non abbiamo preso ... birra.	*non abbyamo prezo beerra*
Is service included?	È incluso il servizio?	*e eenkloozo eel serveetsyo*

sound check

Note the unusual pronunciations of the combinations **gl** and **gn** in Italian.

gl sounds like the 'lli' in 'million':
bottiglia *botteelya*

and **gn** like the 'ny' sound in 'canyon':
gnocchi *nyokkee*
ogni *onyee*

Practise with these words:
famiglia *fameelya*   gli *lyee*
agnello *anyello*   insegnare *eensenyare*

Eating **Out**

order, order
Time to place an order. Complete these sentences using the words on the right.

1 Come _____, prosciutto e melone.
2 Come _____, pasta e fagioli.
3 Come _____, trota alla griglia.
4 Come _____, fagiolini.
5 Come _____, torta al cioccolato.
6 Da _____, prendo una bottiglia di vino rosso.

a primo
b bere
c antipasto
d dessert
e secondo
f contorno

as if you were there
You go to a restaurant one evening. Follow the prompts to play your part in the conversation.

(Greet the waiter and say you'd like a table for two)
Sì. Da bere cosa prendono?
(Ask for a bottle of red wine and a bottle of mineral water)
Va bene. Ecco il menù.
(Thank him and ask what he recommends)
La pizza ai funghi. E anche il risotto di pesce è molto buono.
(That sounds good: order one fish risotto and a mushroom pizza)

Che cos'è il pesto?	**What is** 'pesto'?
Prendo la minestra.	**I'm having** the soup.
Per me le scaloppine.	**For me**, veal escalopes.
Mi porta un po' di pane, per favore?	**Could I have** some bread, please?
Sono vegetariano/a.	**I'm** a vegetarian.
Non posso mangiare i frutti di mare.	**I can't eat** seafood.
Mi può consigliare un buon ristorante?	**Could you recommend** a good restaurant?

saying what you'll have

Ordering food and drink is easy in Italian. Use either Prendo ... or Per me ... followed by the word for 'the' (il, la, i, le) and the dish or drink you want. Remember that the word for 'the' changes according to the gender and number of the item.

Prendo **il** brodetto di pesce. I'll have fish soup.
Prendo **i** petti di pollo. I'll have chicken breasts.
Per me **la** pizza alla rucola. For me, pizza with rocket.
Per me **le** tagliatelle ai funghi. For me, mushroom tagliatelle.

If you want to order an unspecified quantity, use Mi porta ...? (Can you bring me ...?) followed by the word for 'some' (del, della, dei, delle) and the item you want.

Mi porta del pane? Can I have some bread?
Mi porta dei fagiolini? Can I have some green beans?
Mi porta dell'acqua? Can I have some water?
Mi porta delle patatine fritte? Can I have some chips?

Menu **Reader**

courses

antipasto starter
primo first main dish
(pasta or rice)
secondo second main dish
(meat or fish)
contorno side dish
dolce dessert

menus

menù fisso set menu
piatto del giorno dish of the day
specialità della casa speciality
of the house
menù turistico tourist menu

main ways of cooking

affumicato smoked
arrosto roasted
bollito/lesso boiled
alla brace grilled
cotto a vapore steamed
fatto in casa homemade
ai ferri grilled/barbecued
al forno baked
fritto fried
alla griglia grilled
ripieno/farcito stuffed
allo spiedo on the spit
in umido stewed

pasta sauces

aglio, olio e peperoncino
garlic, olive oil and chilli
all'amatriciana tomatoes, red
peppers, bacon, onion, garlic,
white wine
all'arrabbiata tomatoes, chilli,
herbs
al burro butter, parmesan
alla cacciatora onions, wine,
tomatoes, mushrooms,
peppers
alla carbonara bacon, onion,
eggs, cheese
al pesto pine kernels, basil,
garlic, cheese, marjoram
alla pizzaiola tomatoes, garlic,
basil
ai quattro formaggi with four
different cheeses
al ragù tomatoes, minced
meat, onions, herbs
alle vongole clams, tomatoes,
garlic, herbs

the menu

acciughe anchovies
aglio garlic
agnello lamb
alici anchovies

anatra all'arancia duck in orange sauce

antipasto misto selection of cold meats, including ham and salami

aragosta lobster

arancini bianchi/rossi rice balls with cheese/meat filling

asiago fresh mild cheese

asparagi asparagus

baccalà salt cod

basilico basil

bistecca alla fiorentina grilled steak with pepper, lemon juice and parsley

bollito misto mixed boiled meat (mostly Northern Italy)

bruschetta toasted bread, spread with tomatoes, olive oil, oregano, and mushrooms

burro butter

calamari squid

cannelloni pasta tubes

caponata Southern Italian salad of olives, anchovies and aubergines

carciofi artichokes

carne meat

carote carrots

cavolfiore cauliflower

cavolo cabbage

ceci chickpeas

cinghiale wild boar

cipolle onions

coniglio rabbit

costoletta alla milanese veal cutlet in breadcrumbs

cozze mussels

crostini toast, croutons

fagioli haricot or butter beans

fagiolini French beans

farfalle butterfly-shaped pasta

fegato alla veneziana liver fried with onions

fettuccine ribbon pasta

fichi figs

frittata ai funghi/al prosciutto mushroom/ham omelette

fritto misto (di mare) assorted fried fish and seafood

frutti di mare seafood

funghi porcini cep mushrooms

gamberi prawns

gamberetti shrimp

gnocchi dumplings

granchio crab

insalata ... salad

 caprese tomato and
 mozzarella salad with
 oregano and olive oil

 mista mixed

 di pomodori tomato

 verde green

involtini rolled slices of meat
stuffed with ham and sage

lattuga lettuce

linguine flat spaghetti

maccheroni macaroni

maiale pork

mandorle almonds

manzo beef

mascarpone a rich cream
cheese

melanzane aubergines

merluzzo cod

miele honey

mortadella mild spiced salami

mozzarella a creamy cheese

nocciola hazelnut

noci walnuts

olio oil

olive olives

osso buco veal/beef knuckles
cooked in wine and lemon

ostriche oysters

pagliata sweetbreads

panna cream

parmigiano parmesan

pasta e fagioli soup with
noodles and beans

patate potatoes

patatine fritte chips

pecorino sheep's milk cheese

penne tube-shaped pasta

peperonata mixed sweet
peppers

pesce fish

pescespada swordfish

piselli peas

polenta a kind of maize
(boiled, then often fried)

pollo ... chicken

 alla diavola very spicy

 arrosto roasted

 petti di pollo chicken breast

polpo octopus

pomodoro tomato

porri leeks

prezzemolo parsley

prosciutto ... ham

 affumicato smoked

 crudo cured

 cotto cooked

prugne plums

ravioli small filled pasta
squares

rigatoni ribbed tubes of pasta

riso rice

risi e bisi rice with peas and
bacon

risotto ... a rice dish

 alla milanese with saffron
 and white wine

 di pesce with fish

 alla marinara with seafood

rognoni kidneys

rombo turbot

salame salami

salmone salmon

salsicce spicy sausages

saltimbocca alla romana veal
escalope in marsala with ham
and sage

salvia sage
scaloppine small slices of veal
sgombro mackerel
sogliola sole
spezzatino a kind of stew
spigola sea bass
spinaci spinach
sugo sauce
tacchino turkey
tagliatelle ribbon pasta
tartufi truffles
tonno tuna
tortellini small filled pasta shapes
triglia red mullet
trippa tripe
trota trout
uova egg
verdura (mista) (mixed) vegetables
vitello veal
vongole clams
zampone stuffed pig's trotter
zucchine courgettes
zuppa soup

desserts

budino cold custard/chocolate dessert
crostata di mele apple tart
frutta fresca (di stagione) fresh fruit (in season)
(See fruits, p57)
gelato ice cream
macedonia fruit salad
tartufo truffle-shaped vanilla or chocolate ice cream
tiramisù sponge soaked in coffee and alcohol with a mascarpone cream

torta ... cake
  al cioccolato chocolate
  di mandorle almond
zuppa inglese trifle

(For drinks, see pp71, 73, 88)

Entertainment

Local tourist offices should be your first stop for information on cultural and sporting events.

Most of the national newspapers have event listings, and in some larger cities English-language newspapers are available.

sightseeing

Museums and galleries The most popular museums offer advanced ticket purchase, enabling you to avoid long queues. At certain times in the year entrance is free.

Churches Visit churches when there are no services and avoid wearing shorts or short skirts, or showing cleavage or midriff. Check mass times and public opening hours on notices outside the door.

music

Concerts and recitals take place in atmospheric settings such as Verona's outdoor Roman amphitheatre. The Maggio Musicale in Florence, during May, is the oldest Italian music festival. The Umbria Jazz Festival is also popular. For a full-blown opera performance, visit La Scala, Milan and the Teatro San Carlo, Naples.

fairs & festivals

Every village has at least one **festa** (festival) during the year, usually celebrating a saint's day. Famous carnivals are hosted in Venice and Sanremo, in the week preceding the start of Lent. The Palio in Siena, which takes place at the beginning of July and then again in mid-August, is a colourful horse race through the town's narrow streets and squares, dating back to the middle ages.

cinema

Foreign films are usually dubbed, but there are English-language cinemas in the largest towns. The Venice Film Festival takes place at the end of August.

sport

Cycling You can hire bikes in most large towns. The hills of Tuscany and Umbria and the flatlands around the Po delta are popular for cycling.

Football Not so much a national sport as an obsession. Go to a match in any of the big cities to experience pre- and post-match festivities.

Golf Italy has good provision for golfers. To see what's available, check **www.golfeurope.com**.

Horseriding Sometimes offered as part of an **agriturismo** scheme in Tuscany or Umbria.

Motor racing The biggest fixtures are the Grand Prix at Monza, near Milan (September), and San Marino's Grand Prix at Imola (May).

Swimming Beaches are most crowded in August and relatively empty in June and September. Pollution is a continuing problem; check before taking the plunge.

Water sports Scuba diving is good off rocky coasts where the water is clear, for example the islands around Sicily. You can find waterski and windsurf facilities in most large resorts.

Skiing There are accessible slopes in the Alps (from Milan, Turin and Venice); the Abruzzo (from Rome); the Sila and Aspromonte in Calabria and Mount Etna and the Monti Madonie in Sicily.

Tennis The larger hotels have facilities; otherwise ask at the tourist office about public courts.

Walking Nature reserves and national parks have some of the best hiking terrain.

Fishing The inexpensive **permesso di pesca per stranieri**, a licence entitling tourists to fish in Italian waters, is granted by the **provincia**. Many tourist areas offer sea trips with local fisherman.

children

Children are worshipped in Italy and widely welcomed, and it is common to see young children in restaurants until late. **Luna parks** (funfairs) can be found in most cities.

Entertainment

phrasemaker

finding out what's on
you may say ...

Do you have ...	Ha ...	*a*
a map of the town?	una pianta della città?	*oona pyanta della cheetta*
an entertainment guide?	un programma degli spettacoli?	*oon programma delyee spettakolee*
Do you have any information in English?	Ha informazioni in inglese?	*a eenformatsyonee een eengleze*
What is there to see here?	Che cosa c'è da vedere qui?	*ke koza che da vedere kwee*
What is there to do here for children?	Che cosa c'è da fare qui per i bambini?	*ke koza che da fare kwee per ee bambeenee*
Is there ...	C'è ...	*che*
a guided tour?	una visita guidata?	*oona veezeeta gweedata*
bus tour?	un giro turistico?	*oon jeero tooreesteeko*
a football match?	una partita di calcio?	*oona parteeta dee kalcho*
Can you recommend ...	Mi può consigliare ...	*mee pwo konseelyare*
a concert?	un concerto?	*oon koncherto*
an exhibition?	una mostra?	*oona mostra*
a museum?	un museo?	*oon moozeo*
Where is the ... please?	Scusi, dov'è ...	*skoozee dove*
concert hall	la sala concerti?	*la sala konchertee*
cathedral	il duomo?	*eel dwomo*
art gallery	la pinacoteca?	*la peenakoteka*
Are there any ...	Ci sono dei...	*chee sono de-ee*
cinemas?	cinema?	*cheenema*
nightclubs?	nightclub?	*nayt-clab*

you may hear …

Ci sono …	*chee sono*	There are …
le grotte.	*le grotte*	the caves.
due teatri.	*doo-e teatree*	two theatres.
Che cosa le interessa?	*ke koza le eenteressa*	What are you interested in?
Il museo è …	*eel moozeo e*	The museum is …
nella piazza principale.	*nella pyatsa preencheepale*	in the main square.
vicino alla stazione ferroviaria.	*veecheeno alla statsyone ferrovyaree-a*	near the railway station.

check out 1

You go to the tourist office to find out what there is to see in the area.

○ Buongiorno, ha una pianta della città?
bwonjorno a oona pyanta della cheetta

- Ecco a lei.
ekko a le-ee

○ Che cosa c'è da vedere qui?
ke kosa che da vedere kwee

- C'è la Rocca Scaligera e ci sono le grotte di Catullo.
che la rokka skaleejera e chee sono le grotte dee katoollo

○ Ha informazioni?
a eenformatsyonee

- Ecco a lei. C'è una visita guidata della città domani alle dieci.
ekko a le-ee. Che oona veezeeta gweedata della cheetta domanee alle dyechee

○ Grazie.
gratsye

Q There are two main sites to visit: true or false?
What starts at ten o'clock tomorrow?

getting more information

you may say ...

When does it start?	A che ora comincia?	*a ke ora komeencha*
What time does ... finish?	A che ora finisce ...	*a ke ora feeneeshe*
the show	lo spettacolo?	*lo spettakolo*
the match	la partita?	*la parteeta*
How long does it last?	Quanto dura?	*kwanto doora*
What events are on this week?	Che spettacoli ci sono questa settimana?	*ke spettakolee chee sono kwesta setteemana*
When is it open?	Quando è aperto/a?	*kwando e aperto/a*
Do you need tickets?	Ci vuole il biglietto?	*chee vwole eel beelyetto*
Are there any tickets?	Ci sono biglietti?	*chee sono beelyettee*
Where do you buy tickets?	Dove si comprano i biglietti?	*dove see komprano ee beelyettee*
Is there an interval?	C'è un intervallo?	*che oon eentervallo*
Is there wheelchair access?	È accessibile alle sedie a rotelle?	*e acchesseebeele alle sedye a rotelle*
Is it in its original language?	È in versione originale?	*e een versyone oreejeenale*
Does the film have subtitles in English?	Il film ha i sottotitoli in inglese?	*eel feelm a ee sottoteetolee een eenglese*

you may hear ...

Non serve il biglietto.	*non serve eel beelyetto*	You don't need tickets.
È chiuso ...	*e kyoozo*	It is closed ...
alla domenica.	*alla domeneeka*	on Sundays.
in inverno.	*een eenverno*	in the winter.
Lo spettacolo ...	*lo spettakolo*	The performance ...
comincia/finisce alle sette.	*komeencha/ feeneeshe alle sette*	starts/finishes at 7 o'clock.
dura due ore.	*doora doo-e ore*	lasts two hours.
Dalle nove e mezza del mattino alle sette di sera.	*dalle nove e medza del matteeno alle sette dee sera*	From 9.30am to 7pm.

check out 2

You make enquiries about tickets to a concert.

○ Scusi, dov'è la sala concerti?
skoozee dove la sala konchertee

- Nella piazza principale.
nella pyatsa preencheepale

○ Ci vuole il biglietto per il concerto?
chee vwole eel beelyetto per eel koncherto

- No, non serve il biglietto.
no non serve eel beelyetto

○ A che ora finisce?
a ke ora feeneeshe

- Alle 10.50.
alle dyechee e cheenkwanta

Q Where is the concert hall?
Do you need tickets?

Entertainment

buying a ticket

you may say ...

Do you have tickets?	Ha biglietti?	*a beelyettee*
Two tickets, please, for ...	Due biglietti, per favore, per ...	*doo-e beelyettee per favore per*
Saturday.	sabato.	*sabato*
tomorrow.	domani.	*domanee*
Is there a concession for ...	Ci sono riduzioni per ...	*chee sono reedootsyonee per*
students?	studenti?	*stoodentee*
children?	bambini?	*bambeenee*
senior citizens?	anziani?	*antsyanee*
people with disabilities?	disabili?	*deezabeelee*
Where can I buy a programme?	Dove si compra il programma?	*dove see kompra eel programma*
Are the seats numbered?	I posti sono numerati?	*ee postee sono noomeratee*
Is this seat free?	È libero questo posto?	*e leebero kwesto posto*

you may hear ...

Mi dispiace, è tutto esaurito.	*mee deespyache e tootto ezowreeto*	Sorry, it's sold out.
C'è un intervallo di venti minuti.	*chee oon eentervallo dee ventee meenootee*	There's an interval of 20 minutes.
È libero/occupato.	*e leebero/okkoopato*	It's free/taken.
Qui, sulla pianta.	*kwee soolla pyanta*	Here, on the plan.
alla biglietteria	*alla beelyetteree-a*	at the ticket office
il botteghino	*eel bottegeeno*	theatre box office
in lingua originale	*een leengwa oreejeenale*	in the original language
la poltrona	*la poltrona*	seat
la platea	*la platea*	stalls
la galleria	*la galleree-a*	balcony/circle
il palco	*eel palko*	box

check out 3

You decide to take a guided tour of an art gallery.

○ Buongiorno, a che ora comincia la visita guidata?
 bwonjorno a ke ora komeencha la veezeeta gweedata

- Alle undici.
 alle oondeechee

○ Quanto dura?
 kwanto doora

- Un'ora.
 oon ora

○ Quanto costa?
 kwanto kosta

- Otto euro.
 otto e-ooro

○ Ci sono riduzioni?
 chee sono reedootsyonee

- Cinque per i bambini.
 cheenkwe per ee bambeenee

○ Due adulti e due bambini, per favore.
 doo-e adooltee e doo-e bambeenee per favore

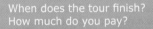

Q When does the tour finish?
How much do you pay?

swimming & sunbathing

you may say ...

Can I use the hotel pool?	Posso usare la piscina dell'albergo?	*posso oozare la peesheena del albergo*
Where are the ... changing rooms? showers?	Scusi, dove sono le ... cabine? docce?	*skoozee dove sono le kabeene doche*
I'd like to hire ... a beach umbrella. a sun lounger.	Vorrei noleggiare ... un ombrellone. una sdraio.	*vorre-ee nolejjare oon ombrellone oona zdrayo*

sports

you may say ...

Where can I play ... tennis? golf?	Dove posso giocare a ... tennis? golf?	*dove posso jokare a tennees golf*
Where can I ... go swimming? go skiing?	Dove posso ... nuotare? sciare?	*dove posso nwotare shee-are*
I'd like to hire ... a racket. waterskis.	Vorrei noleggiare ... una racchetta. degli sci nautici.	*vorre-ee nolejjare oona raketta delyee shee naooteechee*
I'd like to take ... lessons. skiing sailing ice-skating	Vorrei prendere lezioni di ... sci. vela. pattinaggio sul ghiaccio.	*vorre-ee prendere letsyonee dee shee vela patteenajjo sool gyacho*
How much is it ... per hour? per day?	Quanto costa ... all'ora? al giorno?	*kwanto kosta allora al jorno*

you may hear ...

Le lezioni individuali/ di gruppo costano ...	*le letsyonee eendeeveedwalee/ dee grooppo kostano*	Individual/Group lessons cost ...

sports equipment

golf club	la mazza da golf	*la **ma**tsa da golf*
sailing boat	la barca a vela	*la **ba**rka a **ve**la*
skates	i pattini	*ee **pat**teenee*
ski boots	gli scarponi	*lyee skar**po**nee*
skis	gli sci	*lyee shee*
snowboard	lo snowboard	*lo snowboard*
surfboard	la tavoletta da surf	*la tavo**let**ta da surf*
tennis ball	la pallina	*la pal**lee**na*
tennis racket	la racchetta	*la rak**ket**ta*
water skis	gli sci nautici	*lyee shee na**oo**teechee*

check out 4

You want to arrange ski lessons.

○ Vorrei prendere lezioni di sci e noleggiare degli sci.
*vor**re**-ee **pren**dere let**syo**nee dee shee e nolejjare **de**lyee shee*

- Sì, allora le lezioni individuali costano venti euro per un'ora e le lezioni di gruppo costano quindici.
*see **allo**ra le le**tsyo**nee eendeeveed**wa**lee **ko**stano **ven**tee e-**oo**ro per oon ora e le le**tsyo**nee dee **groo**ppo **ko**stano **kween**deechee*

○ E gli sci?
e lyee shee

- Dodici al giorno.
***do**deechee al **jor**no*

Q   How much do individual lessons cost per hour?

sound check

When the consonant following a vowel is doubled, the vowel is short:

palla *palla* ball   pala *pala* spade

The **a** in the second example is slightly drawn out.

When you only have one consonant, the vowel is long.

ecco *ekko* here you are   eco *eko* echo

The **e** in the second example is slightly drawn out.

Practise on these pairs of words: each pronunciation has a very different meaning!

nonno *nonno* grandfather	nono *nono* ninth
tonno *tonno* tuna	tono *tono* tone
fatto *fatto* made	fato *fato* fate

try it out

odd one out

Find the word that doesn't belong in each of these lists.

1 il biglietto, la pallina, il botteghino, il programma
2 l'ombrellone, la piscina, la sdraio, i pattini
3 il duomo, il golf, il calcio, il tennis
4 gli scarponi, i guanti, l'ombrellone, gli sci
5 la barca a vela, la poltrona, il posto in galleria, lo spettacolo

match it up

Match the beginnings and ends to complete these sentences. They're all things you might ask on holiday.

1	Dove ...	a	una racchetta.
2	Che cosa c'è ...	b	lezioni di sci.
3	Vorrei noleggiare ...	c	da vedere qui?
4	Vorrei prendere ...	d	posso nuotare?

as if you were there

You go to the tourist office to find out what's on during your stay. Follow the prompts to play your part.

Buongiorno.
(Greet her and ask if she has a programme of events)
Sì – ecco.
(Thank her and ask what there is to do here)
C'è una visita guidata della città.
(Ask when it starts)
Alle due e mezza.
(Ask if she has any information)
Ecco.
(Thank her and say goodbye)

linkup

<table>
<tr><td>Ha delle informazioni in inglese?</td><td>Do you have any information in English?</td></tr>
<tr><td>Ci vuole il biglietto?</td><td>Do you need a ticket?</td></tr>
<tr><td>Dove si può pescare?</td><td>Where can you fish?</td></tr>
<tr><td>Dove posso giocare a tennis?</td><td>Where can I play tennis?</td></tr>
<tr><td>Mi può consigliare una mostra?</td><td>Can you recommend an exhibition?</td></tr>
<tr><td>Mi piacciono i musei.</td><td>I like museums.</td></tr>
<tr><td>A che ora comincia/finisce?</td><td>What time does it start/finish?</td></tr>
</table>

key phrases

do the right thing

Use si può to find out if you can do something:
Si può noleggiare una canoa qui? Can one hire a canoe here?
Si può prenotare i posti? Can one book seats?

If you see signs saying Non si può ..., it means that a certain activity is prohibited:
Non si può andare in bicicletta nel parco. No cycling in the park.
Non si può fumare. No smoking.

If you want to ask where you can do something, use Dove posso ...? (Where can I ...?):
Dove posso nuotare? Where can I swim?

likes, dislikes & preferences

To say you like or don't like something, use the verb piacere:
Mi piace nuotare. I like swimming. (literally, swimming pleases me)
Non mi piace il golf. I don't like golf.

And if you're talking about more than one thing:
Mi piacciono i film italiani. I like Italian films.

You can show preferences very simply:
Mi piacciono i film americani, ma **preferisco** i film francesi. I like American films, but I prefer French ones.

And you can express stronger feelings:
Mi piacciono molto i film italiani. I like Italian films a lot.
Adoro i film francesi! I adore French films!

Emergencies

reporting crime

Take the usual precautions against pickpockets and don't leave valuables unattended. Personal violence in Italy is extremely rare, and Sicily's much mythologised organised crime is rarely directed against foreigners. The south, however, sees more sexual harassment of women, usually taking the form of staring or comments in the street.

If you are robbed, report the incident to the police as soon as possible, and be sure to get a reference for your insurance claim. Any police officer will help or advise you, though it is the **Polizia** and **Carabinieri** that deal specifically with street crime. **Questure** (police stations) are generally open 24/7 for emergencies, but keep office hours for any other business. If the town you are in does not have a police station and you have been a victim of crime, you may want to visit the nearest **caserma dei carabinieri** (barracks), usually open between 8am and 10pm.

medical treatment

EU nationals must have a valid European Health Insurance Card (EHIC) entitling them to free or reduced cost medical care while in Italy, available online: **www.dh.gov.uk/travellers** or from UK post offices.

In an emergency, dial 118 and ask for **ambulanza** (ambulance) or go to the nearest **ospedale** (hospital) with a **pronto soccorso** (accident and emergency department). Non-emergency treatment can be given at a **farmacia** (chemist's) or by the **ambulatorio** (local health clinic). Most doctors do not operate an appointment service. Just show up and ask who is the last person in the queue.

travellers with disabilities

Facilities for disabled travellers in Italian towns vary enormously. Any Italian Tourist Board or local tourist office can provide a list of hotels which have wheelchair

access. A useful website is **www.disabili.com** (in Italian). The blue badge symbol for disabled car parking is recognised. The major airports offer a service for wheelchair users as do individual airlines, although advance notice is often required.

post offices

Uffici postali (post offices) are marked with a PT against a yellow background. Opening hours are the same as shops. You can buy **francobolli** (stamps) here or in **tabacchini** (tobacconist's).

car breakdown

Motorways have emergency phones every mile or so. Contact your hirer or insurer before travel to find out if they have a reciprocal agreement with an Italian company, as this will work out cheaper than finding a local service once you're there.

telephones

Italy's telephone kiosks take coins or **carte telefoniche** (telephone cards) and some credit cards. Phone cards are available from **tabacchini**. The perforated corner must be removed before use.

Some bars have a public **cabina telefonica** (telephone booth) Ask the barman to give you a line, then make your call and pay afterwards.

useful phone numbers

Police 112
Emergencies 113
(fire, accidents, etc.)
Ambulance 118
Directory enquiries 12
International directory enquiries 170

phrasemaker

emergency phrases

you may say ...

Help!	Aiuto!	*ayooto*
Excuse me! (to attract attention)	Scusi!	*skoozee*
Is there someone who speaks English?	C'è qualcuno che parla inglese?	*che kwalkoono ke parla eengleze*
Leave me alone!	Mi lasci in pace!	*mee lashee een pache*
I'll call the police.	Chiamo la polizia.	*kyamo la poleetseea*
I'm ill.	Sto male.	*sto male*
I need help.	Ho bisogno di aiuto.	*o beezonyo dee ayooto*
I need a ... doctor. ambulance. chemist.	Ho bisogno di ... un medico. un'ambulanza. una farmacia.	*o beezonyo dee oon medeeko oon amboolantsa oona farmacheea*
Can you help me?	Mi può aiutare?	*mee pwo ayootare*
It's urgent.	È urgente.	*e oorjente*

Where is ...	Dov'è ...	*dove*
the police station?	la questura?	*la kwestoora*
the hospital?	l'ospedale?	*lospedale*
Where is the nearest ...	Dov'è il ... più vicino?	*dove eel ... pyoo veecheeno*
petrol station?	distributore di benzina?	*deestreebootore dee bentseena*
garage?	meccanico?	*mekkaneeko*
telephone?	telefono?	*telefono*
Thank you.	Grazie.	*gratsye*

telling the doctor or dentist

you may say ...

I'd like an appointment with a ...	Vorrei un appuntamento con il ...	*vorre-ee oon appoontamento kon eel*
doctor.	dottore.	*dottore*
dentist.	dentista.	*denteesta*
Here's my EHIC.	Questa è la mia tessera sanitaria.	*kwesta e la mee-a tessera saneetarya*
I can't move my leg.	Non posso muovere la gamba.	*non posso mwovere la gamba*
My ... hurts.	Mi fa male ...	*mee fa male*
stomach	lo stomaco	*lo stomako*
foot	il piede	*eel pyede*
My ... hurt.	Mi fanno male ...	*mee fanno male*
eyes	gli occhi	*lyee okkee*
legs	le gambe	*le gambe*
It hurts here.	Mi fa male qui.	*mee fa male kwee*
My ... has a temperature.	Mio/a ... ha la febbre.	*mee-o/a ... a la febbre*
son	figlio	*feelyo*
daughter	figlia	*feelya*
She/He feels sick.	Ha la nausea.	*a la nowzea*
I've got constipation.	Sono stitico/a.	*sono steeteekola*

I've got ...	Ho ...	*o*
diarrhoea.	la diarrea.	*la dyarrea*
a sore throat.	mal di gola.	*mal dee gola*
a cough.	la tosse.	*la tosse*
a headache.	mal di testa.	*mal dee testa*
hayfever.	la febbre da fieno.	*la febbre da fyeno*
I've been sick.	Ho vomitato.	*o vomeetato*
I can't feel my neck.	Non mi sento il collo.	*non mee sento eel kollo*
I've cut myself.	Mi sono tagliato/a.	*mee sono talyato/a*
I've burnt myself.	Mi sono scottato/a.	*mee sono skottato/a*
I've been stung by ...	Mi ha punto ...	*mee a poonto*
an insect.	un insetto.	*oon eensetto*
a jelly fish.	una medusa.	*oona medooza*
I've been bitten by a dog.	Mi ha morso un cane.	*mee a morso oon kane*
I'm allergic to ...	Sono allergico/a agli ...	*sono allerjeeko/a alyee*
antibiotics.	antibiotici.	*anteebeeoteechee*
animals.	animali.	*aneemalee*
I'm diabetic.	Ho il diabete.	*o eel dyabete*
I'm pregnant.	Sono incinta.	*sono eencheenta*
I'm asthmatic.	Ho l'asma.	*o lazma*
I'm epileptic.	Sono epilettico/a.	*sono epeeletteeko/a*
I'm HIV-positive.	Sono sieropositivo/a.	*sono syeropozeeteevo/a*
I have a heart condition.	Sono cardiopatico/a.	*sono kardyopateeko/a*
I have high/low blood pressure.	Ho la pressione alta/bassa.	*o la pressyone alta/bassa*
I have toothache.	Ho mal di denti.	*o mal dee dentee*
I've lost a filling.	Mi è saltata via un'otturazione.	*mee e saltata vee-a oon ottooratsyone*

you may hear ...

Che cosa ha?	ke koza a	What's wrong/What's the problem?
Dove le fa male?	dove le fa male	Where does it hurt?
Sta prendendo altre medicine?	sta prendendo altre medeecheene	Are you on any other medication?
È allergico/a a qualcosa?	e allerjeeko/a a kwalkoza	Are you allergic to anything?
È ...	e	It's ...
una frattura.	oona frattoora	a fracture.
una slogatura.	oona slogatoora	a pulled muscle.
un'intossicazione alimentare.	oon eentosseeka-tsyone aleementare	food poisoning.
L'osso è rotto.	losso e rotto	The bone is broken.
Dobbiamo operare.	dobbyamo operare	You need an operation.
Non è niente di grave.	non e nyente dee grave	It's nothing serious.
Deve ...	deve	You must ...
riposare.	reepozare	rest.
stare a letto.	stare a letto	stay in bed.
bere molta acqua.	bere molta akwa	drink lots of water.
Non deve ...	non deve	You mustn't ...
alzarsi.	altsarsee	get up.
fare movimento.	fare moveemento	take exercise.
Ecco la ricetta.	ekko la reechetta	Here's the prescription.
Le faccio un'otturazione (provvisoria).	le facho oon ottooratsyone (provveezorya)	I'll put in a (temporary) filling.
Devo togliere il dente.	devo tolyere eel dente	I'll have to take the tooth out.

check out 1

You need to see a doctor.

○ C'è qualcuno che parla inglese? Ho bisogno di un medico.
che kwalkoono ke parla eengleze. o beezonyo dee oon medeeko

- Sono un medico. Che cosa ha?
sono oon medeeko. ke koza a

○ Ho bisogno di aiuto. Mia figlia ha mal di gola e mal di testa ...
o beezonyo dee ayooto. mee-a feelya a mal dee gola e mal dee testa

- Vediamo ... Non è niente di grave – un raffreddore. Ecco la ricetta per delle pastiglie per il mal di gola.
vedyamo. non e nyente dee grave – oon raffreddore. ekko la reechetta per delle pasteelye per eel mal dee gola

Q What's the doctor's diagnosis?

Emergencies

at the chemist's

you may say ...

Do you have anything for ...	Ha qualcosa per ...	*a kwalkoza per*
a cold?	il raffreddore?	*eel raffreddore*
a cough?	la tosse?	*la tosse*
diarrhoea?	la diarrea?	*la dyarrea*
sunburn?	l'eritema solare?	*lereetema solare*
constipation?	la stitichezza?	*la steeteeketsa*
burns?	le scottature?	*le skottatoore*
insect stings/bites?	le punture d'insetto?	*le poontoore deensetto*
travel sickness (car, air, sea)?	il mal d'auto, d'aria, di mare?	*eel mal da-ooto, darya, dee mare*
indigestion?	l'indigestione?	*leendeejestyone*
a headache?	il mal di testa?	*eel mal dee testa*
I've got ...	Ho ...	*o*
a fever.	la febbre.	*la febbre*
flu.	l'influenza.	*leenfluentsa*
Can you recommend anything?	Che prodotto mi consiglia?	*ke prodotto mee konseelya*
How often do I have to take it?	Ogni quante ore lo devo prendere?	*onyee kwante ore lo devo prendere*
Does it have side effects?	Ha effetti collaterali?	*a effettee kollateralee*
Do you have any ...	Ha ...	*a*
aspirin?	aspirina?	*aspeereena*
antihistamine?	antistaminico?	*anteestameeneeko*
contact-lens solution?	liquidi per lenti a contatto?	*leekweedee per lentee a kontatto*
condoms?	preservativi/ profilattici?	*preservateevee/ profeelatteechee*
cough mixture?	sciroppo per la tosse?	*sheeroppo per la tosse*
deodorant?	deodorante?	*de-odorante*
nappies?	pannolini?	*pannoleenee*
plasters?	cerotti?	*cherottee*
sanitary towels?	assorbenti?	*assorbentee*
tampons?	assorbenti interni?	*assorbentee eenternee*

you may hear ...

Vuole ...	*vwole*	Would you like...
delle gocce?	*delle gocche*	drops?
della lozione?	*della lotsyone/*	lotion?
della crema?	*della krema*	cream?
delle pastiglie?	*delle pasteelye*	tablets?
Prenda/Applichi ...	*prenda/appleekee*	Take/Apply ...
una/due/tre volte	*oona/doo-e/tre volte*	once/twice/three
al giorno.	*al jorno*	times a day.
prima dei/dopo	*preema dee-e/dopo*	before/after meals.
i pasti.	*ee pastee*	
con acqua.	*kon akkwa*	with water.
Inghiottisca.	*eengyotteeska*	Swallow whole.
Non ...	*non ...*	Don't ...
masticare.	*masteekare*	chew.
succhiare.	*sookkyare*	suck.
Può causare	*pwo ka-oozare*	May cause
sonnolenza.	*sonnolentsa*	drowsiness.
Evitare il contatto	*eveetare eel kontatto*	Avoid contact with
con gli occhi.	*kon lyee okkee*	your eyes.

check out 2

You need to buy something for your diarrhoea.

○ Buongiorno, ha qualcosa per la diarrea?
bwonjorno a kwalkoza per la dyarea

- Ecco. Prenda queste pastiglie tre volte al giorno,
dopo i pasti.
*ekko. prenda kweste pasteelye tre volte al jorno
dopo ee pastee*

○ Grazie.
gratsye

Q How often do you have to take the tablets?

Emergencies

parts of the body

ankle	la caviglia	*la kaveelya*
arm	il braccio	*eel bracho*
back	la schiena	*la skyena*
chest	il petto	*eel petto*
ear	l'orecchio	*lorekkyo*
elbow	il gomito	*eel gomeeto*
eye/eyes	l'occhio/gli occhi	*lokkyo/lyee okkee*
foot	il piede	*eel pyede*
hand	la mano	*la mano*
head	la testa	*la testa*
heart	il cuore	*eel kwore*
hip	il fianco	*eel fyanko*
kidneys	le reni	*le renee*
knee	il ginocchio	*eel jeenokkyo*
leg	la gamba	*la gamba*
mouth	la bocca	*la bokka*
neck	il collo	*eel kollo*
nose	il naso	*eel nazo*
shoulder	la spalla	*la spalla*
stomach	lo stomaco	*lo stomako*
throat	la gola	*la gola*
tooth/teeth	il dente/i denti	*eel dente/ee dentee*

at the police station
you may say …

I've lost my …	Ho perduto …	*o perdooto*
wallet.	il portafoglio.	*eel portafolyo*
passport.	il passaporto.	*eel passaporto*
suitcase.	la valigia.	*la valeeja*
watch.	l'orologio.	*lorolojo*
I can't find my …	Non trovo …	*non trovo*
son.	mio figlio.	*mee-o feelyo*
daughter.	mia figlia.	*mee-a feelya*

I've had my ... stolen.	Mi hanno rubato ...	*mee anno roobato*
watch	l'orologio.	*lorolojo*
bag	la borsa.	*la borsa*
Our car has been broken into.	Ci hanno scassinato la macchina.	*chee anno skasseenato la makkeena*
I was mugged.	Mi hanno scippato.	*mee anno sheepato*
yesterday ...	ieri ...	*yeree*
morning	mattina	*matteena*
afternoon	pomeriggio	*pomereejjo*
last night	ieri notte	*yeree notte*
this morning	stamattina	*stamatteena*
in the street	per la strada	*per la strada*
in a shop	in un negozio	*een oon negotsyo*
It's ...	È ...	*e*
big.	grande.	*grande*
blue.	blu.	*bloo*
expensive.	costosa.	*kostoza*
made of leather.	di pelle.	*dee pelle*

Emergencies

Che cosa è successo?	*ke koza e soochesso*	What happened?
Quando/Dove è successo?	*kwando/dove e soochesso*	When/Where did it happen?
Come si chiama?/ Il suo nome?	*kome see kyama/ eel soo-o nome*	What's your name?
Qual è il suo ... indirizzo? numero di passaporto?	*kwale eel soo-o eendeereetso noomero dee passaporto*	What's your ... address? passport number?
In quale albergo alloggiate?	*een kwale albergo allojjate*	What's the name of your hotel?
Che numero di targa ha?	*ke noomero dee targa a*	What's your car registration?
Deve compilare questo modulo.	*deve kompeelare kwesto modoolo*	Please fill in this form.

valuables

briefcase	la valigietta	*la valeejetta*
digital camera	la macchina fotografica digitale	*la makkeena fotografeeka deejeetale*
driving licence	la patente	*la patente*
handbag	la borsetta	*la borsetta*
jewellery	i gioielli	*ee joyellee*
laptop	il portatile	*eel portateele*
mobile phone	il cellulare/ il telefonino	*eel chelloolare/ eel telefoneeno*
money	i soldi	*ee soldee*
MP3 player	il lettore MP3	*eel lettore emme pee tre*
necklace	la collana	*la kollana*
passport	il passaporto	*eel passaporto*
purse	il portamonete	*eel portamonete*
tickets	i biglietti	*ee beelyettee*
wallet	il portafoglio	*eel portafolyo*

check out 3

Your bag has been snatched. You go to the local police station to report it.

○ Buongiorno, mi hanno rubato la borsa con il portafoglio e il passaporto.
bwonjorno mee anno roobato la borsa kon eel portafolyo e eel passaporto

– Il suo nome?
eel soo-o nome

○ Francesca di Stefano.
francheska dee stefano

– Quando e dove è successo?
kwando e dove e soocchesso

○ Stamattina, per la strada.
stamatteena per la strada

– Deve compilare questo modulo.
deve kompeelare kwesto modoolo

car breakdown

you may say ...

I've broken down.	Ho un guasto alla macchina.	*o oon gwasto alla makkeena*
on the motorway	sull'autostrada	*sooll aootostrada*
... isn't working.	... non funziona.	*non foontsyona*
The engine	Il motore	*eel motore*
The steering	Il volante	*eel volante*
The brakes aren't working.	I freni non funzionano.	*ee frenee non foontsyonano*
I have a flat tyre.	Ho bucato.	*o bookato*

Emergencies

I've run out of petrol.	Sono rimasto/a senza benzina.	*sono reemastola sentsa bentseena*
When will it be ready?	Quando sarà pronta?	*kwando sara pronta*

Qual è il problema?	*kwale eel problema*	What is the problem?
Dov'è?	*dove*	Where are you?
Mandiamo il meccanico.	*mandyamo eel mekkaneeko*	We'll send a mechanic.
Qual è il suo numero di assicurazione?	*kwale eel soo-o noomero dee asseekooratsyone*	What is your insurance number?
Mi faccia vedere i documenti.	*mee facha vedere ee dokoomentee*	Show me your papers, please.
Dopodomani.	*dopodomanee*	The day after tomorrow.
Ripassi più tardi.	*reepassee pyoo tardee*	Come back later.

main car parts

accelerator	l'acceleratore	*lachelleratore*
battery	la batteria	*la batteree-a*
brakes	i freni	*ee frenee*
clutch	la frizione	*la freetsyone*
engine	il motore	*eel motore*
gears	il cambio	*eel kambyo*
radiator	il radiatore	*eel radyatore*
spark plugs	le candele	*le kandele*
steering wheel	il volante	*eel volante*
tyres	i pneumatici	*ee p-neoomateechee*
windscreen	il parabrezza	*eel parabredza*
windscreen wiper	il tergicristallo	*eel terjeekreestallo*

check out 4

You're having trouble with your hire car, and get a mechanic to look at it.

○ Buonasera, ho un guasto alla macchina. Il motore e le luci non funzionano.
bwonasera o oon gwasto alla makkeena. eel motore e le loochee non foontsyonano

- Vediamo ... devo cambiare la batteria e le candele.
vedyamo. devo kambyare la batteree-a e le kandele

○ Va bene. Quando è pronta?
va bene. kwando e pronta

- Dopodomani.
dopodomanee

Q The engine needs replacing: true or false?
The car will be ready tomorrow: true or false?

sound check

As a very general rule, Italian words are pronounced with the stress on the last syllable but one:

motore *motore*   domani *domanee*   sera *sera*

There are many exceptions to this, so it is best to learn where the stress goes as you learn each new word. Note that for words with accents, the stress falls on the accented syllable:

città *cheetta*   caffè *kaffe*   martedì *martedee*

Practise on these words:

campeggio *kampejjo*   economia *ekonomee-a*
lentamente *lentamente*   parmigiano *parmeejano*
ragù *ragoo*   settimana *setteemana*

try it out

odd one out
Find the word that doesn't belong in each of these lists.

1   la testa, lo stomaco, la gola, il distributore di benzina
2   i cerotti, il diabete, l'aspirina, lo sciroppo
3   aiuto! scusi! la ricetta! è urgente!
4   l'otturazione, la macchina fotografica, la borsa, i soldi
5   il medico, l'autostrada, il dentista, la polizia

doctor's orders
Match the ailments on the left to the remedies on the right.

1   Ho la tosse.   a   il cerotto
2   Mi ha punto un insetto.   b   l'aspirina
3   Ho mal di testa.   c   la crema
4   Mi sono tagliato il dito.   d   le pastiglie
5   Ho il raffreddore.   e   lo sciroppo

as if you were there
You're not feeling well, so you go to a chemist. Follow the prompts to play your part.

(Ask if he has anything for a cold)
Ha mal di testa?
(He asks if you have a headache. Say yes, and add that you have a sore throat)
Prenda queste pastiglie, due volte al giorno prima dei pasti.
(Thank him)
Prego.

linkup

key phrases

Mi può aiutare?	**Can you** help me?
Ho bisogno di un medico.	**I need** a doctor.
Mi fa male lo stomaco.	My stomach **hurts**.
Ho la diarrea.	**I have** diarrhoea.
Ha qualcosa per la tosse?	**Do you have anything for** a cough?
Non posso respirare.	**I can't** breathe.
Ho perduto il portafoglio.	**I've lost** my wallet.

where it hurts

If you need to say where something hurts, use mi fa male followed by the word for the part of the body:
Mi fa male la testa. My head hurts.
When referring to more than one part, use mi fanno male:
Mi fanno male gli occhi. My eyes hurt.
Mi fanno male le orecchie. My ears hurt.

something, anything, nothing

Qualcosa **can mean 'something' or 'anything':**
Ha qualcosa per la scottatura? Do you have you anything for a burn?
Vorrei qualcosa per le punture di zanzara. I'd like something for mosquito bites.
And you might get the answer:
Sì, certo. Yes, of course.
No, non abbiamo niente. No, we haven't got anything.

Language **Builder**

Using the words and phrases in this book will enable you to deal with most everyday situations. If you want to go a bit further and start building your own phrases, there are a few rules about Italian that will help you.

gender

All Italian nouns (words for things, people, concepts) are either feminine or masculine. The gender affects the form of 'a' and 'the' used before the noun, as well as any adjectives used with it.

Masculine words usually end in **-o**:

il telefon**o**, il sacchett**o** telephone, bag.

Feminine words usually end in **-a**:

la bottigli**a**, la farmaci**a** bottle, chemist's.

Words ending in **-e** can be either masculine or feminine: you just have to learn these as you go along:

il giornal**e**, la nott**e** newspaper, night.

singular & plural

Nouns change ending when there are more than one of them.

singular nouns ending in ...	in the plural, change to ...
-o	**-i**
-a	**-e**
-e	**-i**

Some examples:

un panin**o**, due panin**i** a bread roll, two bread rolls
una per**a**, due per**e** a pear, two pears
un giornal**e**, due giornal**i** a newspaper, two newspapers
una nott**e**, due nott**i** a night, two nights

words for 'a' & 'the'

These have masculine and feminine forms, and also change before vowels and certain consonants.

	a/an	the (singular)	the (plural)	before ...
masc.	**un** panino **uno** sport **un** anno	**il** teatro **lo** zio **l'**occhio	**i** biglietti **gli** gnocchi **gli** occhi	consonant z, gn, ps, x s + consonant vowel
fem.	**una** birra **un'**edicola	**la** camicia **l'**aranciata	**le** scarpe **le** arance	consonant vowel

talking to people

In Italian, you need to use a different verb form depending on whether you are addressing someone formally or informally. Here are the different ways you would ask 'Do you speak English?':

Parla inglese? (formal, to a stranger or an acquaintance)
Parli inglese? (informal, to a friend, to a child)
Parlate inglese? (plural, to a group of people)

verbs

Verbs in Italian change ending more frequently than in English:
Quanto **costa** il melone? How much does the melon cost?
Quanto **costano** le pere? How much do the pears cost?
Ho il raffreddore. I have a cold.
Mia figlia **ha** il raffreddore. My daughter has a cold.

Language **Builder**

Here is the full present tense of some useful verbs.

parlare:	to speak
parlo	I speak
parli	you speak (informal)
parla	he/she speaks (or formal 'you' speak)
parliamo	we speak
parlate	you speak (plural)
parlano	they speak

andare:	to go
vado	I go
val	you go (informal)
va	he/she goes (or formal 'you' go)
andiamo	we go
andate	you go (plural)
vanno	they go

avere:	to have
ho	I have
hai	you have (informal)
ha	he/she has (or formal 'you' have)
abbiamo	we have
avete	you have (plural)
hanno	they have

essere:	to be
sono	I am
sei	you are (informal)
è	he/she is (or formal 'you' are)
siamo	we are
siete	you are (plural)
sono	they are

dovere:	must/to have to
devo	I must
devi	you must
deve	he/she must (or formal 'you' must)
dobbiamo	we must
dovete	you must (plural)
devono	they must

potere:	can/to be able to
posso	I can
puoi	you can
può	he/she can (or formal 'you' can)
possiamo	we can
potete	you can (plural)
possono	they can

adjectives

An adjective changes form according to whether it refers to a masculine or feminine, singular or plural word. Like nouns, adjectives end in -o, -a or -e in the singular, and -i, -e or -i in the plural.

singular adjectives	plural adjectives
-o	-i
-a	-e
-e	-i

Some examples:

un museo moderno, i musei moderni a modern museum, the modern museums

una mela rossa, le mele rosse a red apple, the red apples

il guanto verde, i guanti verdi the green glove, the green gloves

una borsa verde, le borse verdi a green bag, the green bags

Language **Builder**

As you can see, in Italian, adjectives tend to come after the things or people they describe.

questions

There are two easy ways to ask questions. You can change the word order of a statement:

La banca è aperta. The bank is open.
È aperta la banca? Is the bank open?

Or use the same order, but with a question intonation:

C'è una banca qui vicino. There is a bank near here.
C'è una banca qui vicino? Is there a bank near here?

talking about possession

Di is used to show that something belongs to someone:

la valigia **di** Giovanni Giovanni's suitcase

To talk about 'my book', 'his car' etc, Italian uses the following forms. These change according to the gender of the item possessed, not the gender of the owner.

il suo orologio his or her watch **(because 'watch' is masculine)**
la sua casa his or her house **(because 'house' is feminine)**

	singular		plural	
my	il mio	la mia	i miei	le mie
your	il tuo	la tua	i tuoi	le tue
his/her/your (formal)	il suo	la sua	i suoi	le sue
our	il nostro	la nostra	i nostri	le nostre
your	il vostro	la vostra	i vostri	le vostre
their	il loro	la loro	i loro	le loro

Note that when you're talking about family, you generally drop the word for 'the' in the singular:

mio marito my husband (not il mio marito)

mia sorella my sister (not la mia sorella)

this, that, these, those

These words behave like adjectives, agreeing with the noun in gender and in number (singular or plural):

questo negozio, questi negozi this shop, these shops

questa camera, queste camere this room, these rooms

quel negozio, quei negozi that shop, those shops

quella camera, quelle camere that room, those rooms

saying what you like

To talk about what you like and dislike, you need the phrases mi piace and mi piacciono, from the verb piacere:

Mi piace il vino rosso, non mi piace il vino bianco. I like red wine, I don't like white wine.

Mi piacciono le fragole, non mi piacciono le pere. I like strawberries, I don't like pears.

What the Italian actually says is: 'Red wine is pleasing to me', 'Strawberries are pleasing to me'. So when you're talking about one thing, you use the singular form mi piace and when you're talking about more than one, the plural form mi piacciono.

very much, a lot

When you use molto (very) with an adjective or a verb, it doesn't change form:

La birra è molto buona. The beer is very good.

Costa molto. It costs a lot.

But when you use molto with a noun, it changes depending on the gender and number of the noun (like an adjective):

Non bevo molto vino. I don't drink a lot of/much wine.

Non bevo molt**a** birra. I don't drink a lot of/much beer.
Molt**e** persone parlano francese. A lot of people speak French.
The rules for molto also apply to troppo (too much/too many)
and poco (little).

it, him, her, them

Object pronouns in Italian, i.e. words for 'it', 'him', 'her', 'them'
(lo, la, li, le) change depending on the gender and number of
the nouns they replace:
(il maglione) Lo prendo. I'll take it. (**masculine singular**)
(la borsa) La prendo. I'll take it. (**feminine singular**)
(i biscotti) Li prendo. I'll take them. (**masculine plural**)
(le mele) Le prendo. I'll take them. (**feminine plural**)

prepositions

Prepositions are words like 'in', 'at', 'to'. They play an essential
role in joining words and phrases.

in When referring to a country or a region, regardless of
whether you are in it or going to it, use in:
Sono in Italia in vacanza. I'm in Italy on holiday.
Vado in Umbria in vacanza. I'm going to Umbria on holiday.

a To say you are going to or you live in a town, use a:
Abito a Firenze. I live in Florence.
Vado a Firenze. I'm going to Florence.

da If you need to specify where you are travelling from, use da:
Arrivo da Roma. I've come from Rome.
Il treno va da Londra a Glasgow. The train goes from London
to Glasgow.
Da is also used to talk about shops and services:
Vado dal dentista. I'm going to the dentist's.
Compro una ricarica dal tabacchino. I'll buy a top-up card at
the tobacconist's.

tra/fra You can use tra or fra to mean 'between', 'among' or 'in':

L'ufficio postale è tra la farmacia e la banca. The post office is between the chemist's and the bank.

La Scozia è tra i paesi che parlano inglese. Scotland is among the countries which speak English.

Il treno parte tra dieci minuti. The train leaves in ten minutes.

di Di has a number of useful functions and meanings. You can use it to express belonging:

il passaporto di Anna Anna's passport

È il cellulare di Pietro. It's Peter's mobile.

To talk about where you come from:

Sono di Londra. I'm from London.

And about the contents or the amount of something:

una guida di Milano a guide to Milan

un bicchiere di vino a glass of wine

200 grammi di formaggio 200 grammes of cheese

some/any

There is no distinction in Italian between 'some' and 'any'. To change a statement, e.g. Ha del caffè (You have some coffee) into a question Ha del caffè? (Do you have any coffee?) simply add a question mark.

In Italian, the word for 'some' is made up of the preposition di and the word for 'the', and therefore changes according to gender and number:

Vorrei **del** burro. (masculine singular: di + il)
I'd like some butter.

Vorrei **della** frutta. (feminine singular: di + la)
I'd like some fruit.

Vorrei **dei** pomodori. (masculine plural: di + i)
I'd like some tomatoes.

Vorrei **delle** fragole. (feminine plural: di + le)
I'd like some strawberries.

Answers

Bare Necessities.......

check out
1 false, he asks if you're English; you're staying for one week
2 false, you're a student
3 £1 = €1.50

question time
1c 2e 3b 4a 5d

as if you were there
Buongiorno!
bwonjorno
Mi chiamo Anna, sono di Edinburgo.
mee kyamo anna sono dee edeenboorgo
Sì, sono sposata. Mio marito si chiama James, è scozzese.
see sono spozata. mee-o mareeto see kyama james e skotseze
No, una bambina, Julia.
no oona bambeena julia
Quanti bambini ha?
kwantee bambeenee a

Getting Around.........

check out
1 false, it's right, not left
2 true; yes
3 false, in two stops
4 false, 20 minutes; €35

mind the gap
1d 2c 3e 4a 5b

as if you were there
Due biglietti per Venezia andata e ritorno, per favore.
doo-e beelyettee per Venetsya andata e reetorno per favore
A che ora parte il treno?
a ke ora parte eel treno
È diretto?
e deeretto
A che ora è la coincidenza?
a ke ora e la koeencheedentsa
Grazie.
gratsye

Somewhere to Stay.....

check out
1 two nights; €210
2 no, it's €6 extra
3 you are asked for your room number and to key in your PIN

in the mix
1 cassaforte
2 carta igienica
3 televisore
4 serratura
5 asciugamani

question time
1c/e 2e/c 3d 4f 5a 6b

as if you were there
Buongiorno. Ha una camera doppia con doccia?
bwonjorno. a una kamera doppya kon docha
Per una notte.
per oona nottee
Quanto costa?
kwanto kosta

La prima colazione è inclusa?

*la **pree**ma kola**tsyo**ne e
een**kloo**za*

Va bene, la prendo.

*va **be**ne la **pren**do*

Buying Things..........

check out

1 cherries; false, half a kilo
2 €49; €45
3 2; €23

mind the gap

1d 2c 3b 4a

colouring in

1 rosso
2 verde
3 bianco
4 giallo
5 blu
6 arancio
7 viola
8 nero

as if you were there

Quanto costano (gli occhiali)?

***kwan**to **ko**stano (lyee
ok**kya**lee)*

Ha qualcosa di più economico?

*a kwal**ko**za dee **pyoo**
eko**no**meeko*

Non mi piacciono.

*non mee **pya**cchono*

Mi fa uno sconto?

*mee fa **oo**no **skon**to*

Ci penso, grazie.

*chee **pen**so, **grat**sye*

Café Life...................

check out

1 true; false, €3
2 no, without cream; true
3 €1.50 change (3 x €2 + €1.50)

match it up

CREMA, FRAGOLA, NOCCIOLA,
PISTACCHIO, COCCO

question time

1d 2e 3a 4b 5c

as if you were there

Che gusti ha?

*ke **goo**stee a*

Un gelato alla fragola e uno al
limone.

*oon je**la**to alla **fra**gola e **oo**no
al lee**mo**ne*

In coppetta.

*in ko**ppe**tta*

Ecco ... grazie.

*ekko. **grat**sye*

Eating Out...............

check out

1 true
2 a bottle of sparkling mineral
   water and a bottle of white
   wine

order, order

1c 2a 3e 4f 5d 6b

as if you were there

Buonasera. Un tavolo per due,
per favore.

*bwona**se**ra. un **ta**volo per
doo-e per fa**vo**re*

Una bottiglia di vino rosso
e una bottiglia di acqua
minerale.

*oona botteelya dee veeno
rosso e oona botteelya dee
akwa meenerale*

Grazie. Che cosa consiglia?

gratsye. ke koza konseelya

Un risotto di pesce e una pizza
ai funghi, per favore.

*oon reezotto dee peshe e oona
peetsa aee foongee per favore*

Entertainment.........

check out
1 true; a guided tour of the town
2 in the main square; you don't
   need tickets
3 at twelve o'clock; €26
4 €20

odd one out
1 la pallina
2 i pattini
3 il duomo
4 l'ombrellone
5 la barca a vela

match it up
1d 2c 3a 4b

as if you were there
Buongiorno. Ha un programma
degli spettacoli?

*bwonjorno. a oon programma
delyee spettakolee*

Grazie. Cosa c'è da fare qui?

gratsye. koza che da fare kwee

A che ora comincia?

a ke ora komeencha

Ha informazioni?

a eenformatsyonee

Grazie. Arrivederci.

gratsye. arreevederchee

Emergencies............

check out
1 It's nothing serious – just a
   cold
2 three times a day
3 false, he asks your name and
   when and where it happened;
   you have to fill in a form
4 false, the battery and spark
   plugs; false, the day after
   tomorrow

odd one out
1 il distributore di benzina
2 il diabete
3 la ricetta
4 l'otturazione
5 l'autostrada

doctor's orders
1e 2c 3b/d 4a 5b/d

as if you were there
Ha qualcosa per il raffreddore?

a kwalkoza per eel raffreddore

Sì, e ho mal di gola.

see e o mal dee gola

Grazie.

gratsye

(m) = masculine   (m) = feminine

A

a un/uno/una/un' *oon/oono/oona/ oon*
to be able to potere *potere*
accelerator acceleratore, l' (m) *achelleratore*
to accept accettare *achettare*
adapter riduttore, il *reedoottore*
address indirizzo, l' (m) *eendeereetso*
adult adulto/a, l' (m/f) *adoolto/a*
advanced avanzato/a *avantsato/a*
after dopo *dopo*
afternoon pomeriggio, il *pomereejjo*
after-sun lotion lozione dopòsole, la *lotsyone doposole*
again ancora *ankora*
air conditioning aria condizionata, l' (f) *arya condeetsyonata*
air pump compressore, il *kompressore*
airport aeroporto, l' (m) *a-eroporto*
alarm (wake-up call) sveglia, la *svelya*
all tutto *tootto*
  all you need is basta *basta*
allergic allergico/a *allerjeeko/a*
also anche *anke*
altogether in tutto *een tootto*
always sempre *sempre*
ambulance ambulanza, l' (f) *amboolantsa*
and e *e*
animal animale, l' (m) *aneemale*
ankle caviglia, la *kaveelya*
another altro/a *altro/a*
antibiotic antibiotico, l' (m) *anteebyoteeko*
antihistamine antistaminico, l' (m) *anteestameeneeko*
anyone qualcuno *kwalkoono*
anything qualcosa *kwalkoza*
anything else? altro? *altro?*
apartment appartamento, l' (m) *appartamento*
to apply applicare *appleekare*
appointment appuntamento, l' (m) *appoontamento*
arm braccio, il *bracho*
armchair poltrona, la *poltrona*
arms braccia, le *bracha*
arrival arrivo, l' (m) *arreevo*
to arrive arrivare *arreevare*

artichoke carciofo, il *karchofo*
as far as fino a *feeno a*
ashtray portacenere, il *portachenere*
aside a parte *a parte*
aspirin aspirina, l' (f) *aspeereena*
asthma asma, l' (f) *azma*
at a *a*

B

B&B pensione, la *pensyone*
back schiena, la *skyena*
bacon pancetta, la *panchetta*
bag borsa, la *borsa*
bag borsetta, la *borsetta*
baguette filone, il *feelone*
baked al forno *forno*
baker's panetteria, la /panificio, il *panettereea/paneefeecho*
balcony balcone, il *balkone*
banana banana, la *banana*
bank banca, la *banka*
bar bar, il *bar*
basement seminterrato, il *semeenterrato*
bathroom bagno, il *banyo*
battery (of a car/laptop/mobile phone) batteria, la *battereea*
battery (e.g. torch) pila, la *peela*
battery charger caricabatteria, il /caricatore, il *kareekabattereea /kareekatore*
to be essere *essere*
to be right avere ragione *aver rajone*
beach spiaggia, la *spyajja*
beach umbrella ombrellone, l' (m) *ombrellone*
bed letto, il *letto*
bedroom camera, la *kamera*
beer birra, la *beerra*
before prima di *preema dee*
to begin cominciare *komeenchare*
beginner principiante, il/la *preencheepyante*
behind dietro *dyetro*
belt cintura, la *cheentoora*
bicycle bicicletta, la *beecheekletta*
big grande *grande*
bill conto, il *konto*
biscuit biscotto, il *beeskotto*
to bite (animals/humans) mordere *mordere*
to bite/sting (insects) pungere *poonjere*
bitten morso/a *morso/a*
black nero/a *nero/a*

blanket coperta, la *koperta*
blind persiana, la *persyana*
blood sangue, il *sangwe*
blouse camicia, la *kameecha*
blue blu *bloo*
blueberry mirtillo, il *meerteello*
boat barca, la *barka*
boat battello, il *battello*
boiled bollito/a, lesso/a *bolleeto/a, lesso/a*
bonnet cofano, il *kofano*
book libro, il *leebro*
to book/reserve prenotare *prenotare*
book of tickets blocchetto, il *blokketto*
bookshop libreria, la *leebreeree*
boot scarpone, lo *skarpone*
bottle bottiglia, la *botteelya*
bottom sedere, il *sedere*
box in a theatre palco, il *palko*
bra reggiseno, il *rejjeeseno*
bracelet braccialetto, il *brachaletto*
brake freno, il *freno*
brass ottone, l' (m) *ottone*
breadstick grissino, il *greesseeno*
to break rompersi *rompersee*
breakdown guasto, il *gwasto*
breakfast (prima) colazione, la *(preema) colatsyone*
to breathe respirare *respeerare*
bridge ponte, il *ponte*
briefcase valigietta, la *valeejetta*
to bring portare *portare*
brioche brioche, la *breeosh*
broken rotto/a *rotto/a*
bronchitis bronchite, la *bronkeete*
brooch spilla, la *speella*
broth brodo, il *brodo*
brown marrone *marrone*
brush spazzola, la *spatzola*
bulb lampadina, la *lampadeena*
burn scottatura, la *skottatoora*
to burn (oneself) scottarsi *skottarsee*
to burn bruciare *broochare*
burnt bruciato/a *broochato/a*
bus autobus, l' (m) *owtoboos*
bus stop fermata, la *fermata*
bus tour giro turistico, il *jeero tooreestiko*
business affare, l' (m) *affare*
butcher's macelleria, la *machelleree*

butter burro, il *boorro*
to buy comprare *komprare*

C

cake shop pasticceria, la *pasteecheree*
to call chiamare *kyamare*
to be called chiamarsi *kyamarsee*
camera (digital/disposable) macchina fotografica, la (digitale/usa e getta) *makkeena fotografeeka (deejeetale/ooza e jetta)*
campsite campeggio, il *campejjo*
can (to be able to) potere *potere*
can (tin) lattina, la *latteena*
can I help you? dica?/prego?/ desidera? *deeka/prego/dezeedera*
candle candela, la *kandela*
car macchina, la *makkeena*
car park parcheggio, il *parkejjo*
carafe caraffa, la *karaffa*
caravan roulotte, la *roolot*
cash contanti, i *kontantee*
cashpoint bancomat, il *bankomat*
cassette cassetta, la *kassetta*
castle castello, il *kastello*
cathedral cattedrale, la *kattedrale*
cave grotta, la *grotta*
CD CD, il *chee dee*
centre centro, il *chentro*
ceramics ceramica, la *cherameeka*
chair sedia, la *sedya*
change resto, il *resto*
to change cambiare *kambyare*
changing room cabina, la *kabeena* camerino, il *kamereeno*
cheap economico/a *ekonomeekola*
check controllo, il *kontrollo*
to check controllare *kontrollare*
check-in accettazione, l' (f) *acchetatsyone*
chemist's farmacia, la *farmacheea*
to chew masticare *masteekare*
child bambino, il *bambeeno*
child's bed lettino, il *letteeno*
chin mento, il *mento*
chip patatina fritta, la *patateena freetta*
chocolate cioccolato, il *chokkolato*
chocolate chip (ice cream) stracciatella, la *stracchatella*
Christmas cake panettone, il *panettone*
church chiesa, la *kyeza*

cigarette sigaretta, la *seegaretta*
cinema cinema, il *cheenema*
class classe, la *klasse*
climbing alpinismo, l' (m)
  alpeeneezmo
cloakroom guardaroba, il
  gwardaroba
to close chiudere *kyoodere*
closed chiuso/a *kyoozo/a*
clothes shop negozio di
  abbigliamento, il *negotsyo dee
  abeelyamento*
clutch frizione, la *freetsyone*
coach corriera, la *korryera*
coach pullman, il *poolman*
coat cappotto, il *kappotto*
coconut cocco, il *kokko*
coffee caffè, il *kaffe*
coffee cup tazzina, la *tatzeena*
cold freddo/a *freddo/a*
cold raffreddore, il *raffreddore*
colleague collega, il/la *kollega*
colour colore, il *kolore*
comb pettine, il *petteene*
to come venire *veneere*
commission charge commissione, la
  commeessyone
compartment scompartimento, lo
  skomparteemento
concert concerto, il *koncherto*
condom preservativo, il
  preservateevo
cone cono, il *kono*
connection (travelling) coincidenza,
  la *kooeencheedentsa*
connection (internet) connessione, la
  konnesyone
constipated stitico/a *steeteekola*
constipation stitichezza, la
  steeteeketza
contact lens lente a contatto, le
  lente a kontatto
to contain contenere *kontenere*
copper rame, il *rame*
corner angolo, l' (m) *angolo*
to cost costare *kostare*
cotton cotone, il *kotone*
couchette cuccetta, la *koochetta*
cough tosse, la *tosse*
cough mixture sciroppo per la tosse,
  lo *sheeroppo per la tosse*
cover charge coperto, il *koperto*
cream crema, la *krema*

credit card carta di credito, la *karta
  dee kredeeto*
croissant cornetto, il *kornetto*
to cross attraversare *attraversare*
crossroads incrocio, l' (m)
  eenkrocho
customs dogana, la *dogana*
to cut (oneself) tagliarsi *talyarsee*
cycling ciclismo, il *cheekleezmo*

D

dairy products latticini, i
  latteecheenee
dance hall sala da ballo, la *sala da
  ballo*
dark scuro/a *skoorola*
daughter figlia, la *feelya*
day giorno, il *jorno*
day after tomorrow dopodomani
  dopodomanee
dead end vicolo cieco, il *veekolo
  cheko*
debit card bancomat, il *bankomat*
deck chair sdraio, la *zdrayo*
delicious squisito/a *skweezeetola*
dentist dentista, il/la *denteesta*
department reparto, il *reparto*
departure partenza, la *partentsa*
deposit cauzione, la *kaootsyone*
dessert dessert, il *desser*
to develop sviluppare *sveelooppare*
diabetes diabete, il *dyabete*
diarrhoea diarrea, la *dyarrea*
diesel diesel, il *deezel*
dinghy canotto, il *kanotto*
dinner cena, la *chena*
disabled disabile *deezabeele*
direct diretto/a *deerettola*
disco discoteca, la *deeskoteka*
discount sconto, lo *skonto*
diversion deviazione, la *devyatsyon*
to do fare *fare*
doctor dottore, il/ medico, il *dottore
  medeeko*
doesn't, don't non *non*
done fatto/a *fattola*
don't worry non si preoccupi *non se
  preokkoopee*
door porta, la *porta*
double doppio/a *doppyola*
double bed letto matrimoniale, il
  letto matreemonyale
doughnut bombolone, il *bombolone*
downwards verso il basso *verso eel
  basso*

140

draught (beer) alla spina *alla speena*
to drink bere *bere*
drinkable potabile *potabeele*
driving licence patente, la *patente*
dry secco/a *sekkola*
dustbin cassonetto, il *kassonetto*
DVD DVD, il *dee vee dee*

E

ear orecchio, l' (m) *orekkyo*
earring orecchino, l' (m) *orekkeeno*
Easter cake colomba, la *kolomba*
economics economia, l' (f) *ekonomeea*
elbow gomito, il *gomeeto*
engaged occupato/a *okkoopatola*
engine motore, il *motore*
enjoy your meal! buon appetito! *bwon appeteeto*
envelope busta, la *boosta*
European Health Insurance Card (EHIC) tessera sanitaria, la *tessera saneetarya*
every ogni *onyee*
exchange rate cambio, il *kambyo*
excuse me (informal) scusa *skooza*
excuse me (formal) scusi *skoozee*
excuse me (to get by in a crowded place) permesso *permesso*
exhibition mostra, la *mostra*
exit uscita, l' (f) *oosheeta*
extra a parte *a parte*
eye occhio, l' (m) *okkyo*
eyes occhi, gli *okkee*

F

face viso, il *veezo*
far distante *deestante*
far lontano *lontano*
to feel sentire *senteere*
ferry traghetto, il *tragetto*
festival festa, la *festa*
to fill in compilare *kompeelare*
filling otturazione, l' (f) *ottooratsyone*
film rullino, il/film, il *roolleenol feelm*
fine va bene *va bene*
finger dito, il *deeto*
fingers dita, le *deeta*
to finish finire *feeneere*
finished finito/a *feeneetola*

first primo/a *preemola*
first main dish primo, il *preemo*
fizzy gassato/a *gassatola*
flavour gusto, il *goosto*
flight volo, il *volo*
floor piano, il *pyano*
foot piede, il *pyede*
football calcio, il *kalcho*
football match partita di calcio, la *parteeta dee kalcho*
for per *per*
forehead fronte, la *fronte*
fork forchetta, la *forketta*
form scheda, la *skeda*
4-star petrol super, la *sooper*
free (price) gratuito/a *gratweetola*
free (seat) libero/a *leeberola*
fried fritto/a *freettola*
from da *da*
fruit frutta, la *frootta*
fruit of the forest frutti di bosco, i *froottee dee bosko*
full pieno/a *pyenola*
full board pensione completa, la *pensyone kompleta*
funfair luna park, il *loona park*

G

gallery galleria, la *gallereea*
garden giardino, il *jardeeno*
gentleman signore, il *seenyore*
Gents uomini, gli *womeenee*
to get a flat tyre bucare *bookare*
to get off scendere *shendere*
to get up alzarsi *altsarsee*
glass (drinking) bicchiere, il *beekkyere*
glass (window) vetro, il *vetro*
glasses occhiali, gli *okkyalee*
gloss lucido/a *loocheedola*
glove guanto, il *gwanto*
to go andare *andare*
gold oro, l' (m) *oro*
golf golf, il *golf*
golf club mazza da golf, la *madza da golf*
golf course campo da golf, il *kampo da golf*
good buono/a *bwonola*
good evening buonasera *bwonasera*
good morning buongiorno *bwonjorno*

good night buonanotte *bwonanotte*
goodbye arrivederci *arreevederchee*
green verde *verde*
greengrocer's fruttivendolo, il *froetteevendolo*
grey grigio/a *greejo/a*
grilled alla brace/ai ferri *alla brache/aee ferree*
grocer's negozio di alimentari, il *negotsyo dee aleementaree*
ground floor pianterreno, il *pyanterreno*
group gruppo, il *grooppo*
guidebook guida, la *gweeda*
guided tour visita guidata, la *veezeeta gweedata*
guinea fowl faraona, la *faraona*

H

hair capelli, i *kapellee*
hairdresser's parrucchiere, il *parrookkyere*
hairdryer asciugacapelli, l' (m)/phon, il *ashoogakapellee/fon*
half metà, la *meta*
half mezzo/a *medzo*
half board mezza pensione, la *medza pensyone*
hand mano, la *mano*
hands mani, le *manee*
handle maniglia, la *maneelya*
to happen succedere *soocchedere*
happened successo *soocchesso*
hat cappello, il *kappello*
to have avere *avere*
to have to dovere *dovere*
hayfever raffreddore da fieno, il *raffreddore da fyeno*
head testa, la *testa*
headache mal di testa, il *mal dee testa*
to hear sentire *senteere*
heating riscaldamento, il *reeskaldamento*
heel tallone, il *tallone*
hello (on the phone) pronto *pronto*
hello (informal) ciao *chow*
help! aiuto! *iyooto!*
to help aiutare *ayootare*
to help oneself (self-service) servirsi *serveersee*
here qui *kwee*
here you are ecco *ekko*
high alto/a *alto/a*
hip fianco, il *fyanko*

hire noleggiare *nolejjare*
holiday vacanza, la *vakantsa*
holiday village villaggio turistico, il *veellajjo tooreesteeko*
hospital ospedale, l' (m) *ospedale*
hot chocolate cioccolata, la *chokkolata*
hot caldo/a *kaldo/a*
hotel albergo, l' (m) *albergo*
how come *kome*
how do you do? piacere *pyachere*
how much, how long quanto *kwanto*
humid umido/a *oomeedo/a*
husband marito, il *mareeto*
to hurt fare male *far male*
hydrofoil aliscafo, l' (m) *aleeskafo*

I

ice ghiaccio, il *gyacho*
ice cream gelato, il *jelato*
to be ill stare male *star male*
in fra/tra *fra/tra*
internet café internet café, il *eenternet kafe*
internet point punto internet, il *poonto eenternet*
included incluso/a *eenkloozo/a*
individual individuale *eendeeveedwale*
information informazioni, le *eenformatsyonee*
inside interno/a *eenterno/a*
insurance assicurazione, l' (f) *asseekooratsyone*
to be interested in interessarsi *eenteressarsee*
intermediate intermedio/a *eentermedyo/a*
interval intervallo, l' (m) *eentervallo*
to introduce presentare *prezentare*
iron ferro da stiro, il *ferro da steero*

J

jacket giacca, la *jakka*
jam marmellata, la *marmellata*
jeans jeans, i *jeens*
jeweller's gioielleria, la *joyellereea*
jewellery gioielli, i *joyellee*
job lavoro, il *lavoro*
jumper maglione, il *malyone*
junction incrocio, l' (m) *eenkrocho*

K

key chiave, la *kyave*
to keep tenere *tenere*
kidney rene, il *rene*

kilo chilo, il *keelo*
kitchen cucina, la *koocheena*
knee ginocchio, il *jeenokkyo*
to know sapere *sapere*
knife coltello, il *koltello*

L

lace pizzo, il *peetso*
lady donna, la/signora, la *donna/seenyora*
Ladies donne/signore *donne/seenyore*
lamp lampada, la *lampada*
language lingua, la *leengwa*
laptop (computer) portatile, il *portateele*
to last durare *doorare*
laundry lavanderia, la *lavandereea*
lead piombo, il *pyombo*
to lean out of sporgersi *sporjersee*
leather (hard) cuoio, il *kwoyo*
  (soft) pelle, la *pelle*
to leave partire *parteere*
to leave alone lasciare in pace *lashare een pache*
left sinistra, la *seeneestra*
left-luggage office deposito bagagli, il *depozeeto bagalyee*
leg gamba, la *gamba*
less meno *meno*
lesson lezione, la *letsyone*
letter lettera, la *lettera*
life belt salvagente, il *salvagente*
lifeguard bagnino, il *banyeeno*
lift ascensore, l' (m) *ashensore*
light (colour) chiaro/a *kyaro/a*
light luce, la *looche*
light (car) faro, il *faro*
I like (singular/plural) mi piace/piacciono *mee pyache/pyachono*
line linea, la *leenea*
linen lino, il *leeno*
lips labbra, le *labbra*
liqueur liquore, il *leekwore*
liquid liquido *leekweedo*
litre litro, il *leetro*
local locale *lokale*
lock serratura, la *serratoora*
to look guardare *gwardare*
to lose perdere *perdere*
lost property oggetti smarriti *ojjettee zmarreetee*
low basso/a *basso/a*
luggage bagagli, i *bagalyee*

M

made fatto/a *fatto/a*
magazine rivista, la *reeveesta*
main principale *preencheepale*
to make fare *fare*
marmalade marmellata, la *marmellata*
man uomo, l' (m) *womo*
map of the city piantina, la *pyanteena*
market mercato, il *merkato*
match fiammifero, il *fyammeefero*
match partita, la *parteeta*
me too anch'io *ankeeo*
matt opaco/a *opako/a*
meal pasto, il *pasto*
meat carne, la *karne*
meat sauce ragù, il *ragoo*
meat stock brodo di carne, il *brodo dee karne*
medicine medicina, la *medeecheena*
medium medio/a *medyo/a*
medium (steak) a puntino *a poonteeno*
memory stick schedina di memoria, la *skedeena dee memorya*
men uomini, gli *womeenee*
menu menù, il *menoo*
metre metro, il *metro*
midday mezzogiorno, il *medzojorno*
midnight mezzanotte, la *medzanotte*
milk latte, il *latte*
milk product latticino, il *latteecheeno*
minibar minibar, il *meeneebar*
minigolf minigolf, il *meeneegolf*
minute minuto, il *meenooto*
mirror specchietto, lo *spekkyetto*
to miss mancare *mankare*
Miss ... signorina, la *seenyoreena*
mistake errore, l' (m) *errore*
model modello, il *modello*
money soldi, i *soldee*
more più/ancora *pyoo/ankora*
morning mattina, la *matteena*
motorbike moto, la *moto*
motorway autostrada, l' (f) *aootostrada*
mouth bocca, la *bokka*
to move muovere *mwovere*

MP3 player lettore MP3, il *lettore emme pee tre*
Mr ... signor, il *seenyor*
Mrs ... signora, la *seenyora*
museum museo, il *moozeo*
my mio/a *meeola*

N

name nome, il *nome*
napkin tovagliolo, il *tovalyolo*
nappy pannolino, il *pannoleeno*
natural naturale *natoorale*
nausea nausea, la *naoozea*
near, nearby vicino *veecheeno*
neck collo, il *kollo*
necklace collana, la *kollana*
to need aver bisogno di *aver beezonyo dee*
newsagent's edicola, l' (f) *edeekola*
newspaper giornale, il *jornale*
next prossimo/a *prosseemola*
night notte, la *notte*
nightclub nightclub, il *nayt-clab*
no no *no*
north nord *nord*
nose naso, il *nazo*
not non *non*
  not bad non c'è male *non che male*
  not included escluso/a *eskloozola*
nothing niente *nyente*
number numero, il *noomero*
numbered numerato/a *noomerato*
number plate (car) targa, la *targa*
nylon nailon, il *naylon*

O

office ufficio, l' (m) *ooffeecho*
office clerk impiegato/a, l' (m/f) *eempyegatola*
oil olio, l' (m) *olyo*
olive oliva, l' (f) *oleeva*
one-way senso unico *senso ooneeko*
to open aprire *apreere*
open aperto/a *apertola*
opera opera lirica, l' (f) *opera leereeka*
to operate operare *operare*
opposite di fronte *dee fronte*
orange (colour) arancio/arancione *aranchola ranchone*
orange (fruit) arancia, l' (f) *arancha*
to order ordinare *ordeenare*
original originale *oreejeenale*
outer esterno/a *esternola*

outside fuori *fwooree*
to overtake sorpassare *sorpassare*
over (finished) finito/a *feeneetola*
over there là in fondo *la een fondo*

P

packet pacchetto, il *pakketto*
painting quadro, il *kwadro*
pair paio, il *payo*
palace palazzo, il *palatso*
pardon? come? scusi? prego? *kome/ skooze/prego*
to park parcheggiare *parkejjare*
park parco, il *parko*
passport passaporto, il *passaporto*
pasta pasta, la *pasta*
to pay pagare *pagare*
payment pagamento, il *pagamento*
pea pisello, il *peezello*
pen penna, la *penna*
pensioner pensionato/a, il/la *pensyonatola*
pepper pepe, il *pepe*
performance spettacolo, lo *spettakolo*
perfume shop profumeria, la *profoomereea*
person persona, la *persona*
petrol benzina, la *bentseena*
petrol station distributore di benzina, il *deestreebootore dee bentseena*
photograph foto, la *foto*
pill pillola, la *peellola*
pillow case federa, la *federa*
pillow cuscino, il *koosheeno*
pink rosa *roza*
pistachio pistacchio, il *peestakkyo*
pizza pizza, la *peetsa*
plane aereo, l' (m) *aereo*
plan, map (of town) pianta, la *pyanta*
plaster cerotto, il *cherotto*
plastic plastica, la *plasteeka*
plate piatto, il *pyatto*
platform binario, il *beenaryo*
to play giocare *jokare*
please per favore/per piacere/per cortesia *per favore/per pyachere/per kortezeea*
plug (sink) tappo, il *tappo*
police polizia, la *poleetseea*
police station questura, la *kwestoor...*
port porto, il *porto*
to post spedire *spedeere*
postcard cartolina, la *kartoleena*

prawn gamberetto, il *gamberetto*
pregnant incinta *eencheenta*
prescription ricetta, la *reechetta*
price prezzo, il *pretso*
priority precedenza, la
   prechedentsa
problem problema, il *problema*
programme programma, il
   programma
to pull tirare *teerare*
pulse polso, il *polso*
purple viola *vyola*
purse portamonete, il *portamonete*
to push spingere *speenjere*

Q
quarter quarto, il *kwarto*
quite abbastanza *abbastantsa*

R
racket racchetta, la *rakketta*
radiator radiatore, il *radyatore*
radio radio, la *radyo*
raincoat impermeabile, l' (m)
   eempermeabeele
raisins uvetta, l' (f) *oovetta*
rare (meat) al sangue *sangwe*
raw crudo/a *kroodo*
ready pronto/a *pronto/a*
receipt ricevuta, la/scontrino, lo
   reechevoota/skontreeno
recipe richetta, la *reechetta*
to recommend consigliare
   konseelyare
red rosso/a *rosso/a*
to reduce speed rallentare
   rallentare
reduction riduzione, la
   reedootsyone
registration (car) targa, la *targa*
to remove togliere *tolyere*
rent affitto, l' (m) *affeetto*
to rent prendere in affitto
   prendere een affeetto
to repeat ripetere *reepetere*
to reserve prenotare *prenotare*
rest riposare *reepozare*
restaurant ristorante, il
   reestorante
restaurant car vettura ristorante,
   la *vettoora reestorante*
return ticket andata e ritorno
   andata e reetorno
riding equitazione, l' (f)
   ekweetatsyone

right destra *destra*
ring anello, l' (m) *anello*
risotto risotto, il *reezotto*
road strada, la *strada*
road works lavori in corso *lavoree
   een korso*
roasted arrosto/a *arrosto/a*
room stanza, la *stantsa*
room service servizio in camera, il
   serveetsyo een kamera
to run out of petrol rimanere
   senza benzina *reemanere sentsa
   bendzeena*

S
sachet sacchetto, il *sakketto*
safe cassaforte, la *kassaforte*
safe deposit box cassetta di
   sicurezza, la *kassetta dee
   seekooretsa*
safety belt cintura di sicurezza, la
   cheentoora dee seekooretsa
sailing vela, la *vela*
sailing boat barca a vela, la *barka
   a vela*
salopettes tuta da sci, la *toota
   da shee*
salt sale, il *sale*
sandal sandalo, il *sandalo*
sandwich tramezzino, il
   tramedzeeno
sandwich (toasted) toast, il *tost*
sanitary towel assorbente, l' (m)
   assorbente
sardine sardina, la *sardeena*
satin raso, il *razo*
saucer piattino, il *pyatteeno*
sauna sauna, la *sa-oona*
to say dire *deere*
scarf sciarpa, la *sharpa*
scooter vespa, la *vespa*
seafood frutti di mare, i *froottee
   dee mare*
season stagione, la *stajone*
seat sedile, il *sedeele*
seat posto, il *posto*
second main dish secondo, il
   sekondo
to see vedere *vedere*
   see you (later) ci vediamo *chee
   vedyamo*
   see you tomorrow a domani *a
   domanee*
to send mandare *mandare*

serious serio/a *seryo/a*
service servizio, il *serveetsyo*
set price prezzo fisso, il *pretso feesso*
shampoo shampoo, lo *shampoo*
sheets lenzuola, le *lentswola*
shirt camicia, la *kameecha*
shoe scarpa, la *skarpa*
shoe shop negozio di scarpe, il *negotsyo dee skarpe*
shop negozio, il *negotsyo*
shoulder spalla, la *spalla*
show spettacolo, lo *spettakolo*
shower doccia, la *docha*
side-dish contorno, il *kontorno*
to sign firmare *feermare*
silk seta, la *seta*
silver argento, l' (m) *arjento*
single singolo/a *seengolo/a*
size (of clothes) taglia, la *talya*
size (of prints) formato, il *formato*
size (of shoes) numero, il *noomero*
skate pattino, il *patteeno*
skating rink pista di pattinaggio, la *peesta dee patteenajjo*
ski run pista da sci, la *peesta da shee*
skirt gonna, la *gonna*
skis sci, gli *shee*
sleeping car vagone letto, il *vagone letto*
slice fetta, la *fetta*
slide diapositiva, la *dyapozeeteeva*
to slow down rallentare *rallentare*
slowly lentamente *lentamente*
small piccolo/a *peekkolo/a*
to smoke fumare *foomare*
smoker fumatore, il *foomatore*
soap sapone, il *sapone*
sock calzino, il *caltseeno*
soft drink bibita, la *beebeeta*
sold out esaurito/a *ezaooreeto/a*
someone qualcuno/a *kwalkoono/a*
something qualcosa *kwalkoza*
son figlio, il *feelyo*
sore throat mal di gola, il *mal dee gola*
sorry mi dispiace *mee deespyache*
south sud *sood*
spark plug candela, la *kandela*
to speak parlare *parlare*
speciality specialità, la *spechaleeta*
spoon cucchiaio, il *kookkyay*
square piazza, la *pyatsa*

stadium stadio, lo *stadyo*
stairs scale, le *skale*
stamp francobollo, il *frankobollo*
to start cominciare *comeenchare*
starter antipasto, l' (m) *anteepasto*
station stazione, la *statsyone*
stationer's cartoleria, la *kartolereea*
statue statua, la *statooa*
to stay rimanere *reemanere*
to steal rubare *roobare*
steering wheel volante, il *volante*
stewed in umido *in oomeedo*
still ancora *ankora*
still (water) naturale *natoorale*
sting puntura d'insetto, la *poontoora dinsetto*
stock brodo, il *brodo*
stomach stomaco, lo *stomako*
straight on sempre dritto *sempre dreetto*
to strain (oneself) stancarsi *stankarsee*
street via, la/ strada, la *vee-a/strada*
student studente, lo *stoodente*
to study studiare *stoodyare*
stuffed farcito/a, ripieno/a *farcheeto/a, reepyeno/a*
stung punto/a *poonto/a*
subtitle sottotitolo, il *sottoteetolo*
to suck succhiare *sookkyare*
suede camoscio, il *kamosho*
sugar zucchero, lo *dzookkero*
suitcase valigia, la *valeeja*
sun sole, il *sole*
sunburn eritema solare, l' (m) *ereetema solare*
sunglasses occhiali da sole, gli *okkyalee da sole*
sun cream crema solare, la *krema solare*
supermarket supermercato, il *soopermerkato*
supplement supplemento, il *soopplemento*
surfboard tavoletta da surf, la *tavoletta da serf*
surname cognome, il *konyome*
to swallow ingoiare *eengoyare*
sweater maglione, il *malyone*
sweet caramella, la *karamella*
sweet (adjective) dolce *dolche*
to swim nuotare *nwotare*
swimming costume/trunks costume da bagno, il *kostoome da banyo*

swimming pool piscina, la *peesheena*

T

table tavolo, il *tavolo*
table (for meals) tavola, la *tavola*
tablet pastiglia *pasteelya*
tablecloth tovaglia, la *tovalya*
to take prendere *prendere*
take-away pizza pizza da asporto, la *peetsa da asporto*
to take off/out togliere *tolyere*
taken occupato/a *okkoopato/a*
to take exercise fare movimento *fare moveemento*
tall alto/a *alto/a*
tap rubinetto, il *roobeenetto*
to taste assaggiare *assajjare*
tax tassa, la *tassa*
taxi taxi, il *taksee*
taxi rank posteggio di taxi, il *postejjo dee laksee*
tea tè, il *te*
teaspoon cucchiaino, il *kookyaeeno*
to telephone telefonare *telefonare*
telephone telefono, il *telefono*
telephone card carta telefonica, la *karta telefoneeka*
television set televisione, la *televeezyone*
temperature febbre, la *febbre*
temporary provvisorio/a *provveezoryo*
tennis tennis, il *tennees*
tennis ball pallina, la *palleena*
tennis court campo da tennis, il *kampo da tennees*
tent tenda, la *tenda*
terrace terrazza, la *terratsa*
thank you (very much) grazie (mille) *gratsye meelle*
that quello/a *kwello/a*
that's all, that's enough basta così *basta kozee*
theatre teatro, il *teatro*
theatre box office botteghino, il *bottegeeno*
then poi *poy*
there là *la*
there are ci sono *chee sono*
there is c'è *che*
thigh coscia, la *kosha*
thigh bone femore, il *femore*
to think (believe) credere *kredere*

to think (about) pensare *pensare*
this questo/a *kwesto/a*
throat gola, la *gola*
ticket biglietto, il *beelyetto*
ticket office biglietteria, la *beelyettereea*
tie cravatta, la *kravatta*
tights collant, il *kollan*
till (shop) cassa, la *kassa*
time ora, l' (f) *ora*
timetable orario, l' (m) *oraryo*
tin (e.g. of tomatoes) barattolo, il *barattolo*
tin (e.g. of fish) scatoletta, la *skatoletta*
tissue fazzoletto di carta, il *fatsoletto di karta*
to per *per*
toast crostino, il *krosteeno*
tobacconist's tabacchino, il *tabakkeeno*
today oggi *ojjee*
toe dito, il *deeto*
toes dita, le *deeta*
toilet toilette, la/ gabinetti, i *toylettel gabbeenettee*
toilet paper carta igienica, la *karta eejeneeka*
tomorrow domani *domanee*
too anche *anke*
tooth dente, il *dente*
toothache mal di denti, il *mal dee dentee*
toothbrush spazzolino, lo *spatsoleeno*
toothpaste dentifricio, il *denteefreecho*
toothpick stuzzicadenti, lo *stootseekadentee*
top-up card ricarica, la *reekareeka*
towards verso *verso*
towel asciugamano, l' (m) *ashoogamano*
town città, la *cheetta*
town walls mura, le *moora*
toy shop negozio di giocattoli, il *negotsyo dee jokattolee*
tracksuit tuta sportiva, la *toota sporteeva*
traffic lights semaforo, il *semaforo*
train treno, il *treno*
tram tram, il *tram*
travel agent's agenzia di viaggi, l' (f) *ajentseeya dee vyajjee*

trouser press stiracalzoni, lo *steerakaltsonee*
trouser's pantaloni, i *pantalonee*
to try provare *provare*
to try (taste) assaggiare *assajjare*
T-shirt maglietta, la *malyetta*
tube tubetto, il *toobetto*
to turn girare *jeerare*
tyre gomma, la/ pneumatico, il *gomma/p-neomateeko*

U

underground metropolitana, la *metropoleetana*
underpants mutande, le *mootande*
to understand capire *kapeere*
upwards verso l'alto *verso lalto*
urgent urgente *oorjente*

V

to validate convalidare *konvaleedare*
vase vaso, il *vazo*
vegetarian vegetariano/a *vejetaryano*
velvet velluto, il *vellooto*
very molto *molto*
view of the sea vista sul mare, la *veesta sool mare*
villa villetta, la *veelletta*
vinegar aceto, l' (m) *acheto*
to visit visitare *veezeetare*
visit visita, la *veezeeta*
visitor's tax tassa di soggiorno, la *tassa dee sojjorno*
volleyball pallavolo, la *pallavolo*
to vomit vomitare *vomeetare*

W

waiter cameriere, il *kameryere*
walking marcia, la *marcha*
wallet portafoglio, il *portafolyo*
to want volere *volere*
  I would like vorrei *vorre-ee*
warm caldo/a *kaldo/a*
wash basin lavandino, il *lavandeeno*
washing-up liquid detersivo, il *deterseevo*
watch orologio, l' (m) *orolojo*
water acqua, l' (f) *akwa*
waterbus stop imbarcadero, l' (m) *eembarkadero*
waterbus vaporetto, il *vaporetto*
waterskis sci nautici, gli *shee naooteechee*
way strada, la *strada*
way in entrata, l' (f) *entrata*

to wear (clothes, glasses) portare *portare*
week settimana, la *setteemana*
weekday (adjective) feriale *feryale*
well … allora, dunque … *allora, doonkwe*
well bene *bene*
well done (meat) ben cotto/a *ben kotto/a*
what che *ke*
what (che) cosa *(ke) koza*
wheel ruota, la *rwota*
wheelchair sedia a rotelle, la *sedya a rotelle*
when quando *kwando*
where dove *dove*
which, which one? quale? *kwale*
white bianco/a *byanko*
who, whom chi *kee*
why? perché? *perke*
wife moglie, la *molye*
window finestra, la *feenestra*
window (of a car/train) finestrino, il *feenestreeno*
windscreen parabrezza, il *parabretsa*
windscreen wiper tergicristallo, il *terjeekreestallo*
wine vino, il *veeno*
with con *kon*
without senza *sentsa*
woman donna, la *donna*
wood legno, il *lenyo*
wool lana, la *lana*
to work (function) funzionare *foontsyonare*
to work (job) lavorare *lavorare*
to write scrivere *skreevere*

Y

yellow giallo/a *jallo/a*
yes sì *see*
yesterday ieri *yeree*
yogurt yogurt, lo *yogoort*
you (formal) lei *le-ee*
youth hostel ostello, l' (m) *ostello*

Z

zero zero, lo *dzero, lo*

A

a at, on
abbastanza quite
acceleratore, l' (m) accelerator
accettare to accept, to take
accettazione, l' (f) check-in
aceto, l' (m) vinegar
acqua, l' (f) water
adulto/a, l' (m/f) adult
aereo, l' (m) plane
aeroporto, l' (m) airport
affare, l' (m) business
affittare to let, to rent
affitto, l' (m) rent
agenzia di viaggi, l' (f) travel
  agent's
aiutare to help
aiuto! help!
albergo, l' (m) hotel
aliscafo, l' (m) hydrofoil
allergico/a allergic
allora well, right
alpinismo, l' (m) climbing
alto/a tall, high
altro? anything else?
altro/a another
alzarsi to get up
ambulanza, l' (f) ambulance
anche also, too
anch'io me too
ancora still, again, more
andare to go, to fit
andata e ritorno return ticket
anello, l' (m) ring
angolo, l' (m) corner
animale, l' (m) animal
antibiotico, l' (m) antibiotic
antipasto, l' (m) starter
antistaminico, l' (m) antihistamine
aperto/a open
appartamento, l' (m) apartment
applicare to apply
appuntamento, l' (m) appointment
aprire to open
arancia, l' (f) orange (fruit)
arancio orange (colour)
arancione orange (colour)
argento, l' (m) silver
aria condizionata, l' (f) air
  conditioning
arrivare to arrive
arrivederci goodbye
arrivo, l' (m) arrival
arrosto/a roasted

ascensore, l' (m) lift
asciugacapelli, l' (m) hair-dryer
asciugamano, l' (m) towel
asma, l' (f) asthma
aspirina, l' (f) aspirin
assaggiare to taste, to try
assicurazione, l' (f) insurance
assorbente, l' (m) sanitary towel
attraversare to cross
autobus, l' (m) bus
autostrada, l' (f) motorway
avanzato/a advanced
aver bisogno di to need
aver ragione to be right
avere to have

B

bagagli, i luggage
bagnino, il lifeguard
bagno, il bathroom
balcone, il balcony
bambino/a, il/la child
banana, la banana
banca, la bank
bancomat, il cashpoint
bar, il bar
barattolo, il tin (e.g. of tomatoes)
barca, la boat
barca a vela, la sailing boat
basso/a low
basta all you need, that will do
basta così that's all, that's enough
bastare to be enough
battello, il boat
batteria, la battery
ben cotto/a well done (meat)
bene well
benzina, la petrol
bere to drink
bianco/a white
bibita, la soft drink
bicchiere, il glass
bicicletta, la bicycle
biglietteria, la ticket office
biglietto, il ticket
binario, il platform
birra, la beer
biscotto, il biscuit
blocchetto, il book of tickets
blu blue
bocca, la mouth
bollito/a boiled
bombolone, il doughnut
borsa, la bag
borsetta, la bag

botteghino, il theatre box office
bottiglia, la bottle
braccia, le arms
braccialetto, il bracelet
braccio, il arm
alla brace grilled
brioche, la brioche
brodo (di carne), il (meat) stock
bronchite, la bronchitis
bruciare to burn
bruciato/a burnt
bucare to get a flat tyre
buon appetito enjoy your meal
buonanotte good night
buonasera good evening, goodbye
buongiorno good morning, goodbye
buono/a good
burro, il butter
busta, la envelope

C

c'è (?) there is, is there?
cabina, la changing room
caffè, il coffee
caffè corretto, il coffee with liqueur
caffè americano, il weaker black
  coffee served in a long glass
calcio, il football
caldo/a hot, warm
calzino, il sock
cambiare to change
cambio, il exchange rate, gears
camera, la bedroom
cameriere/a, il/la waiter/waitress
camerino, il changing room
camicia, la shirt, blouse
camoscio, il suede
campeggio, il campsite
campo da tennis, il tennis court
candela, la candle, spark plug
canotto, il dinghy
capelli, i hair
capire to understand
cappello, il hat
cappotto, il coat
caraffa, la carafe
caramella, la sweet
carciofo, il artichoke
caricabatteria, il battery charger
carne, la meat
carta di credito, la credit card
carta igienica, la toilet paper
carta telefonica, la telephone card
cartoleria, la stationer's
cartolina, la postcard

cassa, la till
cassaforte, la safe
cassata, la ice cream with ricotta and
  candied fruit
cassetta, la cassette
cassetta di sicurezza, la safe deposit
  box
cassonetto, il dustbin
castello, il castle
cattedrale, la cathedral
cauzione, la deposit
caviglia, la ankle
CD, il CD
cena, la dinner
centro, il centre, town centre
ceramica, la ceramics
cerotto, il plaster
che what
che cosa what
chi who, whom
chiamare to call
chiamarsi to be called
chiaro light
chiave, la key
chiesa, la church
chilo, il kilo
chiudere to close
chiuso/a closed
ci sono(?) there are, are there?
ci vediamo see you (later)
ciabatta, la ciabatta, slipper
ciambella, la ring doughnut
ciao hello, 'bye (informal)
ciclismo, il cycling
cinema, il cinema
cintura, la belt
cintura di sicurezza, la safety belt
cioccolata, la hot chocolate
cioccolato, il chocolate
città, la town, city
classe, la class
coca-cola, la coke
cocco, il coconut
cofano, il bonnet
cognome, il surname
coincidenza, la connection
colazione, la breakfast
collana, la necklace
collant, il tights
collega, il/la colleague
collo, il neck
colomba, la Easter cake
colore, il colour
coltello, il knife

come how
come? pardon?
cominciare to begin, to start
commissione, la commission charge
compilare to fill in
comprare to buy
compressore air pump
comune communal, common
con with
concerto, il concert
connessione internet, la internet connection
cono, il cone
consigliare to recommend, to advise
contanti, i cash
contenere to contain
conto, il bill
contorno, il side dish
controllare to check
controllo, il check
convalidare to validate
coperta, la blanket
coperto, il cover charge
coppetta, la tub (ice cream)
cornetto, il croissant
corriera, la coach
corso di golf, il golf course
coscia, la thigh
costare to cost
costume da bagno, il swimming costume, trunks
cotone, il cotton
cravatta, la tie
credere to think, to believe
crema, la cream
crema solare, la sun cream
crostino, il toast, crouton
crudo/a raw
cuccetta, la couchette
cucchiaino, il teaspoon
cucchiaio, il spoon
cucina, la kitchen
cuoio, il leather
cuscino, il pillow, cushion

D

da from
dente, il tooth
dentifricio, il toothpaste
dentista, il dentist
deposito bagagli, il left-luggage office

desidera? can I help you? what would you like?
dessert, il dessert
destra right
detersivo, il washing-up liquid
deve you need to, you have to, you must
deviazione, la diversion
di of, from
di fronte opposite
diabete, il diabetes
diapositiva, la slide
diarrea, la diarrhoea
dica can I help you?
dietro behind
dire to say
diretto/a direct
disabile disabled
discoteca, la nightclub
distante far
distributore di benzina, il petrol station
dita, le fingers, toes
dito, il finger, toe
divieto di sosta no parking
doccia, la shower
dogana, la customs
dolce sweet
domani tomorrow
a domani see you tomorrow
donna, la woman, lady
donne Ladies
dopo after
dopodomani the day after tomorrow
doppio/a double
dottore, il doctor
dove where
dovere to have to, to need to, must
dunque well, right
durare to last

E

e and
ecco here you are
economia, l' (f) economics
economico/a cheap
edicola, l' (f) newsagent's
entrata, l' (f) way in
equitazione, l' (f) horseriding
eritema solare, l' (m) sunburn
errore, l' (m) mistake
esaurito/a sold out
escluso/a not included

esterno/a outer
etto, l' (m) 100 grammes

F

farcito/a stuffed
fare to do, to make
fare male to hurt
fare movimento to take exercise
farmacia, la chemist's
faro, il light (car)
fatto/a made, done
fazzoletto di carta, il tissue
febbre, la temperature
federa, la pillow case
femore, il thigh bone
feriale: giorno feriale weekday
fermarsi to stay
fermata, la bus stop
ferri: ai ferri grilled/barbecued
ferro da stiro, il iron
festa, la festival
festivo/a holiday or Sunday
  giorno festivo holiday or Sunday
fetta, la slice
fiammifero, il match
fianco, il hip
figlia, la daughter
figlio, il son
filone, il baguette
finestra, la window
finestrino, il window (of a car / train)
finire to finish
finito/a finished, over
fino a as far as
fioraio, il florist
firmare to sign
forchetta, la fork
forno, il baker's, oven
al forno baked
foto, la photograph
fotografo, il photographer
fra in between
francobollo, il stamp
freddo/a cold
freno, il brake
frittella, la pancake
fritto/a fried
frizione, la clutch
fronte, la forehead
di fronte opposite
frutta, la fruit
frutti di bosco, i fruit of the forest
frutti di mare, i seafood
fruttivendolo, il greengrocer's
fumare to smoke

fumatore, il smoker
funzionare to work
fuochi d'artificio, i fireworks
fuori outside

G

galleria, la gallery, balcony, circle
gamba, la leg
gamberetto, il prawn, shrimp
gassato/a fizzy, sparkling
gelato, il ice cream
ghiaccio, il ice
giacca, la jacket
giallo/a yellow
giardino, il garden
ginocchio, il knee
giocare to play
gioielleria, la jeweller's
gioielli, i jewellery
giornalaio, il newsagent's
giornale, il newspaper
giorno, il day
girare to turn
giro turistico, il bus tour
gola, la throat
golf, il golf
gomito, il elbow
gomma, la tyre
gonna, la skirt
grande big
gratuito free
grazie (mille) thank you (very much)
grigio/a grey
grissino, il breadstick
grotta, la cave
gruppo, il group
guanto, il glove
guardare to look
guardaroba, il cloakroom
guasto, il breakdown
guida, la guidebook
gusto, il flavour

H

ha you have (formal), he/she has

I

ieri yesterday
imbarcadero, l' (m) water bus stop
impermeabile, l' (m) raincoat
impiegato/a, l' (m/f) office clerk
in in, to
in tutto altogether
incinta pregnant
incluso/a included
incrocio, l' (m) crossroads, junction

indirizzo, l' (m) address
individuale individual
informazioni, le information
ingoiare to swallow
interessarsi to be interested in
intermedio/a intermediate
interno/a inner, inside
intervallo, l' (m) interval

J

jeans, il jeans

L

là there
là in fondo over there, down there
labbra, le lips
lampada, la lamp
lampadina, la bulb
lana, la wool
lasciare in pace to leave alone
latte, il milk
latte macchiato, il coffee with lots of milk
latticino, il dairy product
lattina, la can
lavanderia, la laundry
lavandino, il wash basin
lavori in corso road works
lavoro, il job, work
legno, il wood
lentamente slowly
lente a contatto, la contact lens
lenzuola, le sheets
lesso/a boiled
lettera, la letter
lettino, il child's bed, sunbed
letto, il bed
letto matrimoniale, il double bed
lettore MP3, il MP3 player
lezione, la lesson
libero/a free
libreria, la bookshop
libro, il book
linea, la line
lingua, la language
lino, il linen
liquido liquid
liquore, il liqueur
litro, il litre
locale local
lontano far
lozione doposole, la after-sun lotion
luce, la light
luna park, il funfair

M

macchiato, il coffee with just a little milk
macchina, la car
macchina fotografica (digitale), la (digital) camera
macchina fotografica usa e getta, la disposable camera
macelleria, la butcher's
maglietta, la T-shirt
maglione, il sweater, jumper
mal di denti, il toothache
mal di gola, il sore throat
mal di testa, il headache
mancare to miss, to be short of
mandare to send
mani, le hands
maniglia, la handle
mano, la hand
marcia, la walking
marito, il husband
marmellata, la jam, marmalade
marrone brown
masticare to chew
mattina, la morning
mazza da golf, la golf club
medicina, la medicine
medico, il doctor
medio/a medium
meno less
mento, il chin
menù, il menu
mercato, il market
metà, la half
metro, il metre
metropolitana, la underground
mezza pensione, la half board
mezzanotte, la midnight
mezzo/a half
mezzogiorno, il midday
mi dà I'd like …
mi dispiace sorry
minibar, il minibar
minigolf, il minigolf
minuto, il minute
mio/a my
mirtillo, il bilberry
modello, il model
moglie, la wife
molto very
mordere to bite (of animals/ humans)
morso/a bitten
mostra, la exhibition

moto, la motorbike
motore, il engine
muovere to move
mura, le town walls
museo, il museum
mutande, le underpants

N

naso, il nose
naturale natural, still (water)
nausea, la nausea
negozio, il shop
negozio di abbigliamento, il clothes shop
negozio di alimentari, il grocer's
negozio di giocattoli, il toy shop
negozio di scarpe, il shoe shop
nero/a black
niente nothing
no no
noleggiare to hire
nome, il name
non not, don't, doesn't
non c'è male not bad
non si preoccupi don't worry
nord north
notte, la night
numerato/a numbered
numero, il number, size (of shoes)
nuotare to swim

O

occhi, gli eyes
occhiali, gli glasses
occhiali da sole, gli sunglasses
occhio, l' (m) eye
occupato/a taken, engaged
oggetti smarriti lost property
oggi today
ogni every
olio, l' (m) oil
oliva, l' (f) olive
all'ombra in the shade
ombrellone, l' (m) beach umbrella
opera lirica, l' (f) opera
operare to operate
ora, l' (f) time
orario, l' (m) timetable
ordinare to order
orecchino, l' (m) earring
orecchio, l' (m) ear
originale original
oro, l' (m) gold
orologio, l' (m) watch, clock
ospedale, l' (m) hospital

ostello, l' (m) youth hostel
otturazione, l' (f) filling

P

pacchetto, il packet
pagamento, il payment
pagare to pay
paio, il pair
palazzo, il palace
palco, il box (in a theatre)
pallavolo, la volleyball
pallina, la tennis ball
pancetta, la bacon
panetteria, la baker's
panettone, il Christmas cake
panificio, il baker's
panino, il white roll
panino integrale, il wholemeal roll
pannolino, il nappy
pantaloni, i trousers
parabrezza, il windscreen
parcheggiare to park
parcheggio, il car park
parco, il park
parlare to speak
parrucchiera, la hairdresser's
parrucchiere, il hairdresser's
parte: a parte aside, extra
partenza, la departure
partire to leave
partita, la match
partita di calcio, la football match
passaporto, il passport
pasta, la pasta, cake, sweet pastry
pasticceria, la cake shop
pastiglia, la pill
pasto, il meal
patatina fritta, la chip
patente, la driving licence
pattino, il skate
pelle, la leather
penna, la pen
pensare to think (about)
pensionato/a, il/la pensioner
pensione completa, la full board
pensione, la B&B
pepe, il pepper
per to, for
per cortesia please
per favore please
per piacere please
perdere to lose
permesso excuse me (to get by in a crowded place)

persiana, la blind
persona, la person
pettine, il comb
piacere how do you do?, nice to meet you
mi piace, mi piacciono I like
piano, il floor
pianta, la plan, map (of town)
pianterreno, il ground floor
piantina, la map of the city
piattino, il saucer
piatto, il plate, dish
piatto fondo, il bowl (soup)
piazza, la square
piccolo/a small
piede, il foot
pieno/a full
pila, la battery
piombo, il lead
piscina, la swimming pool
pisello, il pea
pista da sci, la ski run
pista di pattinaggio, la skating rink
pistacchio, il pistachio
più more
pizza, la pizza
pizza da asporto, la takeaway pizza
pizzetta, la small pizza
pizzo, il lace
plastica, la plastic
platea, la stalls (in a cinema)
pneumatico, lo tyre
poi then
polizia, la police
polso, il pulse
poltrona, la armchair, stalls seat (in a theatre)
pomeriggio, il afternoon
ponte, il bridge
porta, la door
portacenere, il ashtray
portafoglio, il wallet
portamonete, il purse
portare to bring, to wear (clothes, glasses)
portatile, il laptop
porto, il port
posteggio, il rank (of taxi)
posto, il seat, space
potabile drinkable
potere to be able to, can
precedenza, la priority, right of way

prego? can I help you? what would you like?
prego? pardon? you're welcome
prendere to take
prendere in affitto to rent
prenotare to book, to reserve
presentare to introduce
preservativo, il condom
prezzo, il price
prezzo fisso, il set price
prima colazione, la breakfast
prima di before
primo/a first
primo, il first main dish
principale main
principiante, il/la beginner
problema, il problem
profumeria, la perfume shop
programma, il programme
pronto hello (on the phone)
pronto/a ready
prossimo/a next
provare to try
provvisorio/a temporary
pullman, il coach
pungere to bite/sting (of insects)
puntino: a puntino medium (steak)
punto/a stung
punto internet, il internet point
puntura d'insetto, la sting
può you can (formal), he/she can

Q

quadro, il painting
qualcosa something, anything
qualcuno/a someone, anyone
quale which, which one, what?
quando when
quanto how much, how long
quarto, il quarter
quello/a that
questo/a this
questura, la police station
qui here

R

racchetta, la racket
radiatore, il radiator
radio, la radio
raffreddore, il cold
raffreddore da fieno, il hayfever
ragù, il meat sauce
rallentare to reduce speed, to slow down
reggiseno, il bra

rene, il kidney
reni, le kidneys
reparto, il department
respirare to breathe
resto, il change
ricarica per il cellulare, la top-up
  card (for mobile phone)
ricetta, la prescription, recipe
ricevuta, la receipt
riduttore, il adapter
riduzione, la reduction
rimanere to stay
rimanere senza benzina to run out
  of petrol
ripetere to repeat
ripieno, il stuffing
ripieno/a stuffed
riposare to rest
riscaldamento, il heating
risotto, il risotto
ristorante, il restaurant
rivista, la magazine
roller blade, i roller blades
rompersi to break
rosa pink
rosso/a red
rotto/a broken
roulotte, la caravan
rubare to steal
rubinetto, il tap
rullino film
ruota, la wheel

S
sacchetto, il sachet
sala da ballo, la dance hall
sale, il salt
salvagente, il lifebelt
sandalo, il sandal
sangue, il blood
sangue: al sangue rare (meat)
sapere to know
sapone, il soap
sardina, la sardine
sauna, la sauna
scale, le stairs
scarpa, la shoe
scarpone, lo boot
scatoletta, la tin (of fish)
scendere to get off
scheda, la form
schiena, la back
sci, gli skis
sci nautici, gli water-skis
sciarpa, la scarf

sciroppo per la tosse, lo cough
  mixture
scompartimento, lo compartment
sconto, lo discount
scontrino, lo receipt
scottarsi to burn oneself
scottatura, la burn
scrivere to write
scuro/a dark
scusi excuse me (formal)
sdraio, la deck-chair
secco/a dry
secondo, il second main dish
sedere, il bottom
sedia, la chair
sedia a rotelle wheelchair
sedile, il seat
semaforo, il traffic lights
seminterrato, il basement
sempre always
sempre dritto straight on
senso unico one-way
sentire to hear, to feel
sentirsi to feel
senza without
serio/a serious
serratura, la lock
servirsi to help oneself (self-service)
servizio, il service
servizio in camera, il room service
seta, la silk
settimana, la week
shampoo, lo shampoo
sì yes
sicurezza, la security
sigaretta, la cigarette
signor, il Mr ...
signora, la Mrs ..., lady
signore, il gentleman
signorina, la Miss ..., young lady
singolo/a single
sinistra, la left
snowboard, lo snowboard
soldi, i money
sole, il sun
sole: al sole in the sun
sorpassare to overtake
sottotitolo, il subtitle
spalla, la shoulder
spazzola, la brush
spazzolino, lo toothbrush
specchio, lo mirror
specialità, la speciality
spedire to post

spettacolo, lo show, performance
spettacolo del pomeriggio, lo
  matinée
spiaggia, la beach
spilla, la brooch
alla spina draught (beer)
spingere to push
sporgersi to lean out
squisito/a delicious
stadio, lo stadium
stagione, la season
stancarsi to strain
stanza, la room
stare to stay, to be
stare male to be ill
statua, la statue
stazione, la station
stitichezza, la constipation
stitico/a constipated
stomaco, lo stomach
stracciatella, la chocolate chip (ice
  cream)
strada, la street, road, way
studente, lo student
studiare to study
stuzzicadenti, lo toothpick
succedere to happen
successo happened
succhiare to suck
sud south
super, la 4-star petrol
supermercato, il supermarket
supplemento, il supplement
sveglia, la alarm, wake-up call
sviluppare to develop

T

tabacchino, il tobacconist's
taglia, la size (of clothes)
tagliarsi to cut oneself
tallone, il heel
tappo, il plug (sink)
targa, la registration/number plate
tassa, la tax
tassa di soggiorno, la visitor's tax
tavola, la table
tavoletta da surf, la surfboard
tavolo, il table
taxi, il taxi
tazzina, la coffee cup
te, il tea
teatro, il theatre
telefonare to telephone
telefono, il telephone

telefono a scatti, il private pay
  phone
televisore, il television set
tenda, la tent
tenere to keep
tennis, il tennis
tergicristallo, il windscreen wiper
terrazza, la terrace
tessera sanitaria, la EHIC
  (European Health Insurance Card)
testa, la head
tirare to pull
toast, il toasted sandwich
togliere to take off/out, to remove
toilette, la toilet
tosse, la cough
tovaglia, la tablecloth
tovagliolo, il napkin
tra in, between
traghetto, il ferry
tram, il tram
tramezzino, il sandwich
treno, il train
tubetto, il tube
tuta da sci, la salopettes
tuta sportiva, la tracksuit
tutto all
  in tutto altogether

U

ufficio, l' (m) office
umido/a humid
  in umido stewed
un po' a bit
uomini, gli men, Gents
uomo, l' (m) man, gentleman
urgente urgent
uscita, l' (f) gate, exit
uvetta, l' (f) raisins

V

va it/he/she goes
va bene I'm/It's fine
vacanza, la holiday
vagone letto, il sleeping car
valigia, la suitcase
valigietta, la briefcase
vaporetto, il waterbus
vaschetta, la (large) tub
vedere to see
vediamo let's see
vegetariano/a vegetarian
vela, la sailing
vengono they come, they cost
venire to come, to cost

verde green
verso towards, about
verso il basso downwards
verso l'alto upwards
vespa, la scooter
vetro, il glass
vettura ristorante, la restaurant car
via, la street
vicino near, nearby
vicolo cieco, il dead end
viene comes, costs
villaggio turistico, il holiday village
villetta, la villa
vino, il wine
viola purple
visita, la visit, tour
visita guidata, la guided tour
viso, il face
vista sul mare, la view of the sea
volante, il steering wheel
volere to want
volo, il flight
vomitare to vomit
vorrei I'd like
vuole(?) you want, do you want?
  (formal)

Y
yogurt, lo yogurt

Z
zero, lo zero
zucchero, lo sugar